EMPOWERING NETWORKS

Computer Conferencing in Education

EMPOWERING NETWORKS

NETWORKS

Computer Conferencing in Education

Michael D. Waggoner
University of Northern Iowa
Editor

1992

EDUCATIONAL TECHNOLOGY PUBLICATIONS
ENGLEWOOD CLIFFS, NEW JERSEY 07632

Library of Congress Cataloging-in-Publication Data

Empowering networks : computer conferencing in education / Michael D.
   Waggoner, editor.
      p. cm.
      Includes bibliographical references (p.   ) and index.
      ISBN 0-87778-238-5 : $34.95
      1. Education--United States--Data processing. 2. Education.
   Higher--United States--Data processing. 3. Computer conferencing-
   -United States. 4. Computer networks--United States. I. Waggoner,
   Michael.
   LB1028.43.E47   1992   91-27151
   370'.285 --dc20   CIP

Printed in the United States of America.

Library of Congress Catalog Card Number:
91-27151.

International Standard Book Number:
0-87778-238-5.

First Printing: January 1992.

To my family
Rita, Joanna, and Joel
my personal empowering network

Introduction

Michael D. Waggoner

Computer networks are increasing in their availability and sophistication to the point that they are empowering individuals and groups in new productive educational relationships. By networks, we mean the computer-mediated communication technologies of electronic mail and computer conferencing. The latter is of particular interest. While the interaction of individuals has been expedited by electronic mail, it is computer conferencing—the use of the computer to facilitate group work independent of time and space constraints—that presents the major opportunities for empowerment.

The technology of computer conferencing has existed for many years. It has been only during the last five years, however, that the proliferation of microcomputers and concomitant interest in new applications of the computer have heightened interest in computer-mediated communication—from local area networks to international networks. Technical advances and reduced costs have contributed to this growth of interest and innovation.

The purpose of this book is to capture the experience of some of the major, unique applications of computer conferencing that have been developed in education to date. By describing a wide range of successful uses of this technology, two objectives are served: to encourage further experimentation, and to provide some collected wisdom regarding implementing and maintaining such an enterprise. Such an effort must necessarily be selective, because even at this early stage, many projects have evolved. We have chosen representative applications in the three general areas of educational work: teaching, research, and service. Additionally, we have invited two seasoned practitioners with experience in computer conferencing to reflect broadly on issues of implementation and change in educational organizations.

Chapter One discusses the use of computer conferencing as an integral component of the mission of the Office of Professional Development at the University of Michigan School of Education in the early 1980s. One of the early major computer conferencing systems, Confer, was developed at Michigan in the mid-1970s. Consequently, there was a technical infrastructure in place from which a program of services designed for external constituents of the school was developed. The authors chart the development of these wide ranging applications from their inception. **Dr. Christine Canning** is Assistant Professor of Education at the University of Northern Iowa; she was a coordinator in the Office of Professional Development and helped initiate and manage some of the applications mentioned. **Dr. Karen Swift** is an Assistant Professor of Education at Central Michigan University; she coordinated student teacher placement at Michigan for a time and worked with the use of this medium with the student teachers.

In Chapter Two, authors describe how the University of Virginia Curry School of Education embraced computer conferencing in the 1980s with the aim of adding an electronic dimension to their founder Thomas Jefferson's notion of an "academical village." The important idea of culture is discussed when introducing this medium into the life and work of an education organization. **Dr. Glen Bull** is Associate Professor of Instructional Technology at the Curry School of Education. **Dr. Judi Harris** is field coordinator of the Teacher-LINK project, also at Virginia. **David Drucker** is Coordinator of the Educational Technology Center at the Curry School of Education.

The experience of Western Montana College's Big Sky Telegraph is related in Chapter Three. Developed initially as a resource to the large number of Montana rural educators, this system has grown into a multifaceted operation bringing people together across wide geographic distances. **Dr. Frank Odasz** is Assistant Professor of Computer Education at Western Montana College and is Director of Big Sky Telegraph.

Chapter Four focuses on a teaching application of this technology at The Open University in Milton Keynes, England. The Open University implemented computer conferencing in connection with the delivery of a multimedia distance education course. The author reviews the rationale for this first introduction of the technology into this situation and examines the effects and implications of the experience. **Mr. Anthony Kaye** is with the Institute of Educational Technology at The Open University in Milton Keynes, England.

The use of computer-mediated communication in instructional gaming and simulation is the subject of Chapter Five. The author discusses the use of computer conferencing to enhance and transform the capacities of these teaching strategies. The chapter traces early applications on the University of Michigan campus to the involvement of hundreds of schools across the United States and internationally. **Dr. Frederick L. Goodman** is Professor of Education at the University of Michigan, School of Education. He contributed to the creation of computer conferencing in the mid-1970s.

Chapter Six relates the evolving use of national and international mail networks and conferencing by educators in the forms of the CompuServe Educational Research Forum and BITNET. The author recounts the establishment of the resource exchange on the commercially available CompuServe Information System and the use of BITNET to facilitate exchange among university based educators. **Dr. Jean W. Pierce** is Professor of Education at Northern Illinois University; she helped found the educational research forum on CompuServe.

The next two chapters explore the potential for this medium to facilitate research. In Chapter Seven, the Rural Teacher-Researcher Project is discussed. This involved a partnership of the North Central Regional Educational Laboratory, the Bread Loaf School of English at Middlebury College in Vermont, and Unison Telecommunications Services in Ohio. This project combined a summer residence program with academic year computer conferencing and facilitated research collaborations among participants.

Dr. Lawrence B. Friedman of the North Central Regional Educational Laboratory and **James McCullough**, a teacher of English from Petoskey, Michigan, co-authored the chapter.

Chapter Eight reviews the use of computer conferencing in a structured decision making process to conduct a modified delphi to forecast technology developments in education. **Dr. Michael D. Waggoner** is Associate Professor of Higher Education and Director of Technology at the University of Northern Iowa, College of Education.

The final two chapters bring the reflections of two seasoned practitioners to bear on the promise and potential of this technology in education. **Dr. Don McNeil** brings his rich experience in distance education to a discussion in Chapter Nine of the causes for delay in wider scale adoption of computer conferencing. He reviews his experiences with this medium at the New York Institute of Technology and now as Senior Program Officer at the Academy for Educational Development in Washington, D.C.

Dr. Thomas J. Switzer caps off this collection with thoughts on empowering for technological change. Taking advantage of the opportunities available through computer conferencing requires attention to change strategies in education organizations. In this chapter, the author reviews what we know about change from research and practice and combines that with his perspective as a Dean of a large and complex College of Education. **Dr. Switzer** is Dean of the College of Education at the University of Northern Iowa.

This project was accomplished with the substantial assistance of three people whose work deserves acknowledgment and many thanks. We agreed to use desktop publishing to produce the camera ready copy of the manuscript. A great number of hours were required for scanning chapters into machine readable form, formatting, and editing. Doug Kilian was the first to help in this process. Elizabeth Fischer continued and concluded the book. There throughout the process was Don Luck, providing the needed guidance and wizardry at the appropriate moments. My genuine thanks to these three helpful and conscientious people.

Table of Contents

xi

1

Connecting the University and the Field of Practice: Computer Conferencing in Education at The University of Michigan

Christine Canning and Karen Swift

This chapter reviews the computer conferencing activities that evolved during the 1980s as the Office of Professional Development sought to implement its vision of electronically linking educators from higher education and the field of practice. Field-based educators were actively encouraged to join the on-going conversations "hosted" by The University of Michigan on its computer conferencing system. There, university and public school people began to talk together about a variety of topics of mutual interest related to the improvement of educational practice.

For this university professional school, computer conferencing came to be seen as a powerful medium for collegial conversations. It would be useful for maintaining links with graduates and associates, for disseminating information from the research institution, and for identifying and exploring issues that were surfacing out in the field of practice that might be addressed in university-based research, teaching, or service. By 1984, computer conferencing had become one of the main activities of a unit in the School of Education's Office of Professional Development.

Beginnings

The Office of Professional Development was created in 1981. Its mission was to provide ways to narrow the traditional "gap" between those in the research institution and those in the field

1

of practice. School of Education administrators believed that bringing university faculty and practitioners together in interactive partnerships was a critical task of the professional school. Facilitating such collaborative activities that could result in professional growth for all participants was the role assigned to the Office of Professional Development. Early in its evolution, the office saw a unique role for technology in facilitating its mission. A brief description of the computer conferencing system will precede the discussion of how computer conferencing was used to implement this vision in both inservice and preservice professional development.

The Confer Computer Conferencing System

Various technologies surfaced in the early 1980's with exciting potential for education at Michigan. One was the Confer® computer conferencing system developed at Michigan in the 1970's by Robert Parnes during his doctoral study. His work in computer conferencing arose out of his interest in the psychology of group dynamics, and he designed Confer to implement principles of collegial and democratic interaction.

A Confer user belongs not to the Confer system at large but to various, specific groups of his or her choice. Each group has a purpose or special interest, its own conference facilitator, and a group of people whose names and introductions are kept in a conference roster accessible to each group member.

While there is a private message facility on a Confer conference, the most powerful feature of the system is the public discussion feature. Each public discussion appears as an item that is accessible to all members of the group. Participants can respond to each item as many times as they like over days, months, or even years. Each time a participant joins the group, i.e., signs on to the conference, he or she is told by Confer of any new messages, items, and/or responses to items that have been added since the last sign-on. At the command "new," Confer presents this material, stopping after each entry so the participant can make a response, delete the entry from his or her file, or save it for future reference or action.

Confer resides in the Michigan Terminal System (MTS) on the Ann Arbor campus. MTS can handle hundreds of conferences, many thousands of users in total, and hundreds of users at a time. It is accessible via the MERIT network with a local telephone call from a growing number of cities in Michigan and from Washington, D.C., as well as through computer networks available throughout the world.

The current Confer model is Confer II. Its developer continues to make improvements on this system, and the University supports projects to enhance its presentation and use.

The Vision

Confer captured our imaginations. It provided a way to do what we had always wanted to do, create professional networks among university and public school educators. Such networks could be used in a variety of ways to facilitate professional growth.

Workshop participants could stay in touch with each other and with their directors and professors as they went "back home," often alone, to implement new ideas and their various action plans. University faculty involved in consultant relationships with local school districts could participate in ongoing planning, follow-up support, and consultation. Those interested in various public educational programs and legislation could have immediate access to information and technical assistance, and state department consultants, for example, could have immediate access to those they served. Professional organizations whose members were scattered around the state could carry on discussions between their face-to-face meetings, setting agendas, exploring issues, and making announcements and requests.

Educational leaders could exchange information to help them make various decisions in areas such as capital expenditures, school management, and curriculum development. Those who felt "isolated," a physics teacher, for example, who might be the only one in that content area in a school or district, could be in touch with peers and consultants for curriculum ideas, reflection about various practices in use, problem-solving, and social interaction. Access to human resources with a range of interests, backgrounds, and fields of expertise could benefit any user.

In a world where workshops and inservice training were being done more and more by educational agencies outside higher education, inviting educators to use the university's Confer system for their professional conversations gave Michigan something unique and useful to offer in the professional development market-place. Interested educators could "come to Michigan" to discuss pressing issues, to solve educational problems, and to utilize and learn about powerful new educational technologies. For School of Education faculty and students, Confer could provide increased opportunity for interaction with practitioners for program improvement.

Getting Started

Several forces were working for us as we began. Computer conferencing had been working in the university community for several years. Confer was a system that already had a life and history. One conference, a project of the university's Center for Research on Learning and Teaching (CRLT) that is described below, became a resource in our implementation effort. CRLT:Micros had many participants and daily conversations that were sources of information about technology and its social dynamics.

We participated in this conference to hone our Confer skills, and we planned to introduce our clients to this group. We also started our own conferences to experiment with using the system to meet our communication needs within our unit and the School of Education.

Human resources were of vital importance. One human resource was the leadership in the Dean's office. Both the Dean and

Associate Dean were advocates of networking, and they were both Confer users. They used the system extensively, on and off line they encouraged others to use it, and they were excited about the potential this technology had to address existing needs in education and professional development. These leaders took a risk. They created and continued a structure to support this innovation that had potential for long-term impact but little promise for immediate and highly visible results.

The staff appointed to work in the Office of Professional Development were people who were excited by new technologies, who were inclined to learn and use them, who had experience with the phenomenon of change in the school setting, and who were given time and resources dedicated to the development of the Confer project. This staff included a director and manager responsible for strategic planning and development; a secretary who maintained records and Confer accounts both on and off line; a technical expert who provided assistance in response to innumerable questions from clients related to hardware, software, and telephone problems; and liaisons between the university and various local, state, and national educational communities.

University faculty and staff outside the Office of Professional Development also became resources both on and off line. A critical value shared among our human resources was respect for open channels of communication and distributed accessibility patterns among participants. That is, each Confer participant had direct access to every other participant, and information was shared without gatekeepers.

University resources also included equipment. There were computers of various kinds on desks in the Office of Professional Development and in its computer room. In addition, there were multiple computers for training in facilities around the university and equipment to take home for after-hours exploration and work. Telephone lines and connections were installed as needed.

In 1983, the Office of Professional Development initiated its Confer service to make Confer available to professionals outside the University of Michigan and to promote the use of computer conferencing within the School of Education as a way to link the higher education community to those in the field of practice.

Generally speaking, the Office of Professional Development worked with three types of conferences. First, there were the public conferences already under way within the university community that were open to our clients. Second, we opened both public and private conferences for our client groups to use for their own purposes. Finally, we maintained conferences that were used by School of Education faculty for their collaborative activities with practitioners.

Public Conferences of the University Community

CRLT:Micros has been and continues to be the largest, most active Confer group on the University of Michigan host system. As of August 1989, it was nearing the end of its ninth volume in its ten-year history. When it reaches the size of around 900 items, a new volume is started, and print copy of the retiring volume is made available at a public resource center on campus. From April of 1988, when it was started, until August of 1989, CRLT:Micros9 had 794 participants who had spent just over 9000 hours in conference activity, an average of about ten hours per participant over the seventeen-month period. It has been estimated that 30-40% of the participants are from outside the University of Michigan.

The focus of CRLT:Micros is computer technology used in the university setting. Discussions are terse, highly technical, and useful to participants. The author of Item 821, for example, wanted information on how to scan a picture from a magazine into a PC Paintbrush format. In the list of twenty responses, he was given suggestions of ways to do this task, the technologies that he might want to use, where these technologies were available on campus, and how to access them if he wasn't a faculty member or student, what not to use and why, alternative ways to do the task, things to think about in relation to scanning, estimated costs, and tricks from another's experience. All this in a matter of a day or so.

As with other conferences, most user activity is reading. Comparing the number of items and responses *made* with the number of items and responses *seen*, only about 1% of the public discussion activity is writing. Unlike other conferences, more is written in public items in CRLT:Micros than in private messages. The ratio of public item and response entry to private message entry is about five to one.

Karl Zinn, one of the CRLT:Micros conference managers, offers the following guidelines that are illustrative of mature Confer use :

1. Expect others to be helpful.
2. Be casual about spelling and grammar.
3. Make responses relevant and useful.
4. Enter short items which fit on the screen or on a page of paper.
5. Use more than one item to present different topics for discussion.
6. Post public items whenever possible instead of private messages.
7. Convert useful messages to items to share with others.
8. Use the Confer index to help you find what you need.
9. Enter a new item to ask for help in finding information.
10. Use FORGET to tell Confer which items are not of interest to you.
11. Make use of printed copy shelved on campus, or make your own.
12. Use <Control-E> or <Break> to skip text you don't want to see (Zinn, 1989a).

In another item, he adds these additional points of good Confer etiquette:

1. Participate under your own name.
2. Enter responses which add to the substance of the conference. For example, simply confirming what's said in an early item only makes it "active" again and calls it to everyone's attention.
3. Contribute to public discussions expecting some participant to quote you or otherwise draw information from the conference as if it were a public meeting.
4. Respect the informal nature of some items and responses, considering it conversation not intended for print, in contrast to (3). Ask permission before quoting; give contributors a chance to explain their position.
5. Respect the intentions of other participants, recognizing that the medium of the keyboard and alphanumeric screen tends to filter out important parts of communication otherwise conveyed by tone of voice and facial expression.
6. Review your own entries to be sure they represent your real intentions. Consider adding *emphasis* or a smile. :>) And if you are upset or angered by another's entry, perhaps it's best to wait a while before you respond. (Would you say it to his/her face, in front of others?) (Zinn, 1989b).

In 1984, CRLT opened another public conference to focus more narrowly on computing in the field of education, CRLT:EdMicros. This conference became a forum for discussion across the higher education community and the public schools, a popular place for educators interested in computing in education to meet and interact. Discussion was less technical and more related to instructional concerns. When it was just over three years old, it had 436 participants who had spent about 1300 hours there.

Of all the public conferences using Confer on the UM system, this conference was probably the most successful in terms of providing a meeting ground for university and public school representatives for substantive discussion on topics of mutual interest. CRLT closed this conference, however, in 1989 after opening CRLT:Design, a conference representing its newer interest in software design and intelligent tutoring systems.

About a dozen other conferences on the UM system are also available to anyone with a computer account. Over half of these are for discussions about various technologies, such as CRLT:Mac.notes for discussion about the Macintosh computer. Several are for discussion about Confer, and a few are for discussions on topics other than technology. Meet:Ourselves was opened in June of 1989 for the promotion of good health, and as it has turned out, more social interaction among Confer users. Informal conversations about physical, emotional, and social health here are carried on by people across a range of the professions. From June 1989 to January 1990, almost 200 participants were active for an average of over five hours each.

These conferences have histories that are evidence that computer conferencing can indeed be useful and well used for collegial interaction. We hoped for similar success with our Confer projects in the Office of Professional Development. When it was decided to invite educators out in the field of practice to "join us" at Michigan to utilize Confer for professional development, our dream was that communication among them as well as with those in the university community would proliferate in ways that had before not been possible.

Conferences for Groups External to the University

Of the several hundred conferences established by the Office of Professional Development, most were for educational agencies that wanted to use Confer for their own purposes among members of their own groups. We began with a few groups who had promise as Confer adopters since they were already users of technology and had communication needs that could be met with computer conferencing. These groups also had interests in education that were relevant to interests and work of faculty, staff, and students associated with the School of Education.

REMC Conferences

The first group outside the University to adopt Confer with the help of the Office of Professional Development included the twenty-two directors of the state's Regional Educational Media Centers (REMC). These people were early users and advocates of various media, including computers, in their own settings, and they had a need to communicate with each other from their locations around the state of Michigan. They were used to organizing the sharing of resources, and they wanted to be in touch with their Michigan Department of Education contact person who was also on Confer.

It was determined that the REMC directors would have a private conference for their own work, EDPD:REMC, and another conference, REMC:Forum, as a public conference for discussion of topics of general interest open to any interested educator. The conference management responsibilities were to be shared by REMC members and Office of Professional Development staff members.

For this initial group, the orientation and training were carefully planned. Groups of REMC directors were brought to campus for orientation to Confer and training on the terminals in one of the Computing Center facilities. Excitement was high, but there were some hurdles.

Learning to use Confer on the campus terminals that were already directly connected to the UM Host was easy. The hard part, in these early days, was getting to the UM system by telephone from back home, where there were varieties of computers, modems, and communications software programs. There was always something new to learn about equipment. Another hurdle was participants' lack of access to a computer in their own back home situations. The computer needed to be in a place where the user could use it as a matter of easy routine and where there was a wall jack to a dedicated telephone line. These conditions were not as common then as now.

Even when these conditions were met, there were other hurdles. In these early days, the UM Host was reached via MERIT with a local telephone call in a limited number of locations. Those outside these areas had to contend with long distance telephone charges. These were days of idiosyncratic problem-solving.

The REMC Directors were pioneers. Many managed the early hurdles, and their conferences have experienced steady use and growth over the seven years of their lives to date. About 20% of the activity in REMC's public conference occurred in its fifth year. Its almost 500 participants included public school administrators, consultants from intermediate and local school districts, teachers, and representatives from various universities.

In conference activity lasting about 1200 hours over the first five years, there have been 7000 messages sent, 1700 public discussion entries made, and 58,000 public discussion entries displayed to users. Much of the talk was about technology in the beginning. In the fifth year, however, 83% of the items were requests for help, with more than half of these having to do with curriculum and instructional materials, not computers. A small number of items had to do with employment opportunities and various things for sale or needed by districts. About 10% of the conference items were announcements about public meetings and inservices, and 7% were conversations having to do with philosophical issues and policy.

REMC:Forum became known as a place to get in touch with those in the general education community, but except for the Deans and the Office of Professional Development staff and associates, members of the higher education community seldom joined the conversations there.

Recently one of the REMC directors commented on his experience in the private conference. "Computer conferencing has been *very* useful," he said. "We saved up to a day's meeting time last month by identifying and discussing major issues on EDPD:REMC before our annual planning meeting in Traverse City. When we got there, we could get right to the meat of things, right on task. Especially on items that need some reflection, the discussions that happen over time on the conference render better results than those we do in a hurry when we're together on limited time at a meeting."

MACUL Conferences

The Michigan Association for Computer Users in Learning (MACUL) adapted this concept to a pair of conferences, then expanded it to several. Although MACUL board members were avid users and advocates of computing technology from both higher education and public schools throughout the state, computer conferencing for them was new, and the full implementation took several years.

In 1985 after discussion over a year's time in several face-to-face meetings, MCUL:Board was opened as a private conference for board members. In 1986, MCUL:SIGCC was opened as a public conference of the Special Interest Group for Computer Coordinators (SIGCC). That same year, a group of Logo enthusiasts who had their own conference, LOGO:Forum, became a MACUL special interest group, and MACUL took their conference into its group of conferences. In 1987, the board opened several private conferences, one for each of its working committees and one for the MACUL Newsletter staff. Of these, the most useful was MCUL:CONF, which was used for planning and administration of the annual meeting by the MACUL chairpersons and the continuing education agency that had a contract with MACUL for this service.

Conference management in all these groups was a shared responsibility among MACUL board members. One of these board members was also a member of the Office of Professional Development staff who provided an annual Confer workshop at a fall board meeting as well as on-line assistance and frequent in-person encouragement to her board colleagues. When computer conferencing was widely used among board members, it was cost effective for the organization and its members. Long distance telephone charges were decreased, and members saved the time they'd previously spent playing "telephone tag" with each other.

In 1988, MCUL:Forum was opened as a public conference for MACUL members and others interested in educational computing. This conference was less active than others in the MACUL group, at least in terms of public discussion. It may be that those who wanted to participate in computer conferencing were already doing so on the other MACUL conferences. In fact, most of the MCUL:Forum participants were also MCUL:SIGCC participants. While the hope was that the public forum would attract more of the general membership, most of the general membership were public school teachers. Networking has not been a need or custom for teachers in the same way it was for district computer coordinators. Modems were not common peripherals for classroom teachers to have either at school or at home, and school access to a dedicated telephone line was not available in most schools.

The private board conference seems to have been the most used of the MACUL conferences. It also appears that the MACUL conference which might have been the most fertile meeting ground for university faculty and practitioners was MCUL:SIGCC. Of the participants in this conference, however, a small number were indeed university representatives. While there were more University faculty who perceived themselves as active resource persons to MACUL than there were to any other professional organization in the state, most faculty activity with MACUL involved making face-to-face presentations at the annual meeting.

Other Conferences Outside the University Community

From 1984 to 1988, the Confer universe supported by the Office of Professional Development mushroomed to include more than three hundred conferences and over two thousand users. A relatively small number of these users became active in public forum discussions. MSTA:Forum and MICH:Gifted are two examples.

MSTA:Forum is a public conference sponsored by the Michigan Science Teachers Association for science teachers. Two active members who are Confer enthusiasts and who have existing professional relationships with University science education faculty serve as conference managers in this group. MSTA recently made grants of computer modems to members who said they would prompt and participate in ongoing discussions, and members have become involved in computer conferencing projects that include public school student activity.

Discussion items covered a variety of topics including astronomy, computers, elementary science, jobs, laboratory safety, awards and scholarships, curriculum, events and calendars, journals, philosophy, science fairs, textbooks, and teacher training. While most participants in this conference are public school teachers, there is also involvement from University faculty, staff, and students in science education.

MICH:Gifted serves as a communication link between the Michigan Department of Education's consultant for Gifted Education, who is the conference manager, and consultants around the state. On a one-time basis, funding was allowed for the purchase of computer modems for participation in this and other telecommunications projects.

Most text in MICH:Gifted is posted as information to be disseminated from the MDE. Several items have featured discussion designed to help MDE personnel create useful guidelines for funding programs with their constituents. Other items have focused on location of resources and on issues such as grade skipping and what happens after school for students in programs for the gifted. Virtually none of this discussion included members of the university community.

Most conferences established by the Office of Professional Development for groups outside the University were private, open only to members of the client group. A conference established for a Department of Education curriculum project is an example. During the summer of 1989, twelve persons, some from higher education and some from public schools, were contracted by the Michigan State Department of Education to prepare a curriculum document under the direction of Bill Yarrock at Michigan Technological University in the Upper Peninsula. The writers were from various locations across the state, time was limited, and funding for travel was limited. Although the writers were not expert computer users, it was decided to use Confer as a writing tool for this project.

Each page in the document was conceived as a conference item. Writers entered the pages, i.e., items, for which they were responsible, and others made comments as responses. The editor downloaded this material from the conference to his own word processor for editing and brought hard copy of the first draft to the first face-to-face meeting for in-person discussion. Other rounds of writing and editing followed.

Did working on a computer conference contribute to the success of this project? According to the project director Bill Yarrock: "Very much so. We could not have finished the document in the time we had without it." Other groups did not experience such feelings of tangible success when they opened conferences as membership forums rather than for a specific task to accomplish in a given period of time.

Many different things have happened with the conferences established for groups outside the University. Some started with excitement, promise, and fanfare and then faded away quietly. Some never took off at all. Some struggled but never quite made it. Some had active, highly useful lives with the pace and duration set by a particular task. Some have had slow, steady activity over the years. In some, waves of activity alternated with periods of inactivity. In a few others, activity was constant and, for the most part, dependent on a relatively small number of Confer "regulars."

Much of the talk has been about technology, especially in the early years when many Confer users were the serious computer enthusiasts who were eager to try the new technology and to talk about others they were approaching and/or using. Computer conferencing was a good medium to exchange technical information about specific questions related to using the new, multi-faceted technologies that were proliferating in a rapidly changing marketplace. Those conversations continue.

Other conversations have evolved, too. Conferences have been used by those with a common professional interest for general "lounge" talk and by work groups with a specific task or agenda. People have explored ideas, and they have solved administrative problems. They have interacted with people they would have not otherwise met, and they have enriched connections with people they already knew. Participants have collected data about a wide range of things from their Confer colleagues. They have planned projects, meetings, and conferences, evaluated them, and accomplished follow-up activities. They have exchanged information, and they have acted as support groups.

In groups where there was discussion that was philosophical in nature, it either was routed for some action, was used by individual participants, or was abandoned. For example, points from a discussion on MSTA:Forum about the purpose of science teaching were contributed by one of the conference managers to a Michigan Department of Education K-12 science curriculum development project. A discussion in LOGO:Forum on the question "Is LOGO dead?" generated fifty-six responses among ten participants, including a LOGO developer living in Canada, five university people from two different universities, three local district computer resource people, and one county computer consultant.

This discussion was used for at least one journal article and was quoted by the various participants on a number of occasions.

Confer was a useful tool for data gathering on topics of high interest among a Confer group's users. A participant who wanted help exploring how a new University program prepared leaders in educational technology, for example, collected a wealth of ideas from MCUL:SIGCC members who wanted to contribute to making university preparation programs more relevant to needs in the field. In many of the more intellectual conversations that were not relevant to current issues in the participants' lives or to decisions for some immediate action, the last discussion response was often a question left unanswered.

Almost all these conferences were dependent on autonomous, self-directed action of the users. While there were a few attempts to provide some equipment, training, and on-site technical assistance to members, few organizations "mandated" the use of computer conferencing, providing the necessary resources to an appropriate number of people, and then using the medium for critical information that was not reiterated elsewhere. Organizations made conferences available for those who were interested and motivated to use them on their own initiative. What happened was the result of the perceived fit of conferencing to needs, norms, and resources of the individual users. If it fit, people used it. If it did not fit, it was generally ignored. If it was ignored by most of the people in a group, the early enthusiasts usually talked among themselves for a while and then returned to the more traditional means of communication that were being used by most of their peers.

Inside the university community, interested faculty members were given equipment, technical support, and informal encouragement. The deans were personal models for the use of Confer to participate in collegial discussions with practitioners in public forums. Yet such use never became a priority of most of the faculty. Staff and graduate students in technology programs were more active and visible than were faculty across the public conferences. It could have been a matter of faculty not having time to take from academic work that was already defined, narrowly focused, and demanding. Also, for those faculty who did not already have collegial relationships with the practitioners with whom they could communicate in these forums or who had no specific task of mutual interest on which to focus, venturing into these public forums just may never have seemed like the thing to do.

Whatever the reason, except for a few Confer champions, School of Education faculty generally did not enter public conference forum groups to interact with practitioners. With regard to our goal of bridging the gap between higher education and the field of practice in conferences established on the UM system by professional organizations outside the University, we were disappointed. While professional development did indeed happen on UM system conferences, and the networking that occurred was perceived as empowering to the users, the university was generally the supplier of the computer host and not an integral part of the interaction. Interactions on conferences established by university units, on the other hand, were not so disappointing.

School of Education Conferences

Conferences initiated by School of Education faculty have been more successful in terms of bringing together School of Education faculty and practitioners. While the participant lists in these conferences are not as large as in the public conferences, the quality and per capita level of participation is quite high.

EDPD:Hrtfd was a private conference for the Hartford School District and Michigan staff and faculty who were on a team of consultants engaged in a three-year project in this district across the state from the University. Although district personnel who used the system had to do so on a long-distance telephone call, they had cost-effective, ongoing access to their university consultants. Confer interaction was also an environment for social networking and the building of relationships among the participants that improved the quality of the communication that occurred as a part of the project.

Items were used to arrange meetings and deadlines, to discuss issues that surfaced, and to exchange information related to the project.

Perhaps the most successful Confer project in the School of Education in terms of numbers of participants and in terms of its impact on improvement in the teacher education program in the School were the conferences established among student teachers, teacher education faculty, and a cadre of practitioners appointed to work with the University in teacher education. These conferences also involved people who came to the project as computer novices and met needs that existed long before the advent of computing technology.

MICH:TeacherEd

It has long been recognized that the student teaching term is one of the most critical and stressful aspects of preparation to become a teacher. Student teachers are in a kind of "never never land" as they are no longer students in the way that they once were, but they also are not quite teachers. They feel a lack of identity. Some have described the feeling as that of being like "second-class citizens." They are overwhelmed with the amount of work required and wonder if anyone else has to work as hard as they.

At the University of Michigan the student teaching-related seminar helped to alleviate some of the stress caused by such feelings as it provided a forum whereby students could discuss with one another and a University supervisor some of the problems they encountered and feelings they experienced during their student teaching days. The brevity of the seminar and the necessity to include discussion of pedagogical and other education-related issues, however, limited the amount of time that could be devoted to individual student needs. We were, thus, looking for a way of increasing the contact of students with people who could give them some help and offer some assurance. We wanted to reduce the isolation of our student teachers by increasing their opportunities to interact with their peers and with a variety of professionals in the field and at the University.

Toward that end, the School of Education, during the Winter/Spring 1987, purchased 300 computer terminals and modems that could be used for networking by student teachers and education professionals. In addition, approximately 60 outstanding teachers and administrators from the surrounding districts were invited to become members of a special Cadre (Professional Teacher Corps) and receive appointments as adjunct faculty. Among the Cadre members' responsibilities would be to serve as an advisory group to the School of Education and as "mentors" for student teachers.

In the summer of 1987, we called a planning meeting of faculty, staff, and Cadre teachers who were available during the summer. At that meeting we planned the Confer II training for those new to computer conferencing and determined the initial focus of the conference that would begin with student teachers in the fall. We also decided that Cadre members and School of Education faculty and staff should have their own conference—MICH:EdCorps— and that its content should begin with lighter issues and be allowed to evolve more substantive content spontaneously, which it quickly did.

That summer, we had five workshops in which we trained 36 people in the use of Confer II. We also encouraged those who did not have computers at home to check out one of our computer terminals to use throughout the school year. Several took advantage of the offer.

Unfortunately, at that point some of our problems began, problems that were to plague us a number of times during that first term. Teachers left the workshops with a feeling of excitement— of eagerness to begin communicating with one another by means of this newly learned medium. Even those who were most resistant seemed ready. Some, however, arrived home with their computers and were unable to deal with the technical aspects of setting them up. In several cases, it wasn't their lack of "know how," but, rather, faulty equipment that was the problem. For several, who were computer shy to begin with, this was all the deterrent that was needed. One teacher did not let us know for four months that she had been unable, even after several telephone calls to Media Services, to get the computer into operation. She indicated that she thought that it was her ineptness, so she was too embarrassed to contact us to let us know. We did find that her terminal was not usable, but we were never able to win her over to computer conferencing after that discouraging episode.

Such problems were in the minority. Many of those who had attended workshops and some who had prior knowledge of and previous involvement in computer conferencing signed into MICH:EdCorps, thus beginning a conference that continues today to offer an active forum in which teachers and University faculty and staff discuss current and salient issues related to K-12 education and to pre-service and in-service teacher education. By fall 1987, about 25 teachers and University teacher education faculty and staff were relatively proficient in using Confer. We were ready to expand our computer conferencing network to the 83 student teachers who had field placements for the fall term.

Having done a survey of the student teachers, we knew that substantial training was going to be needed. Only about 35 percent felt competent in the use of computers and Confer. About 50 percent had minimal experience with computers and no experience in the use of Confer, and some had no computer experience at all. Several workshops, at various levels, enabled students to begin at a level most appropriate to them. Although participation in Confer was a requirement, attendance at the workshops was not.

MICH:TeacherEd was to be a conference in which student teachers could communicate with one another, with classroom teachers and school administrators, and with University faculty and staff. We kicked-off the conference by posing several items and requiring student teachers to respond to them as part of their seminar work. As participants began introducing items, the conference quickly took on a life of its own with very little help from its organizers. By the end of the Fall term, 126 participants (83 student teachers, 24 professional teachers, and 19 University teacher education faculty and staff) had generated a total of 106 items, 2013 responses, and 2813 messages.

The extent of the Fall computer conference began, even as early as October, to become unwieldy. Although there was an index, participants felt compelled to try to read all new items and responses. As a consequence, in the Winter term, we retained MICH:TeacherEd for education topics that were generic in nature and then initiated other conferences that pertained to the subject areas/grade levels (art, elementary, English, foreign language, mathematics, music, physical education, science, social studies) in which the students were working. MICH: StuTchr, a conference that was off-limits to all but student teachers, also was created and, according its organizer, had very lively participation.

If quantity is accepted as a measure of success, the extended format of the Winter term conferences proved to be extremely successful. The following table shows approximate figures comparing the Fall and Winter terms:

	FALL MICH:TeacherEd	WINTER MICH:TeacherEd	Subject/Grade Level
Participants	128	151	*148 +
Items	106	114	279
Messages	2813	2223	*466 +
Hours of Use	782	745	*325 +

*Corresponding figures from the social studies conference were unavailable and thus are not reflected here. There were at least 23 social studies student teachers, however, all of whom were required to participate in this subject area conference.

Even though some data from the Winter term are not included, it is obvious that there was a considerable increase in usage when comparing the Winter and Fall terms. While there were

106 items generated during the Fall term, there was a total of 393 items generated in the student conferences during the Winter term. Participants in the Winter conferences were involved in conferring for at least 7 hours on average as compared with 6.1 hours during the Fall. This Winter participation time does not include the number of hours taken to generate the 89 items and many responses in the social studies conference—a factor that could raise the average considerably.

One of the purposes originally promulgated for instituting the computer conferencing among student teachers was to bridge the communication gap among disciplines. To a great degree the Fall conferences succeeded in doing that as all students were seeing and responding to the same items. There was some question, as a result, as to whether we would re-create the gap by having separate subject/grade level conferences. Because this was a concern, we encouraged students to "look in" on conferences that were not for their specific subject areas. Much to our delight, many students not only "looked in" but also participated fully in several of the conferences, thereby contributing added dimensions to the perspectives expressed in various items and responses.

Item topics in the conferences ranged from student teachers organizing social functions to such weighty issues as helping students deal with death and suicide among their peers and in their families and with the teacher's responsibilities in handling suspected child abuse. Other issues, such as the meaning of literacy and how to foster it and whether tracking is useful and effective, appeared in each term's conferences. The most prevalent themes, however, were those of teaching strategies, classroom activities, student motivation, and classroom management. As the school terms drew to a close, the discussions about education seemed to take a more philosophical direction, and these aspiring teachers also began expressing concern about their job searches—résumé writing, interviewing, and job availability among other topics.

An important motivation for creating these computer conferencing networks was to permit professional teachers, student teachers, and University faculty and staff of various backgrounds to interact and discuss questions about teacher preparation and to provide a system of support for student teachers. The worth of the network was once again proven as student teachers were given support in discussions on how to deal with their feelings of being "second-class citizens" and their anxieties about the future. One student introduced an item that expressed those anxieties so vividly: "I was thinking last night, wow! We are all graduating soon. That's pretty scary in itself. Then I wondered am I really ready to have a classroom of my own? Will I be able to handle it? Do any of you feel this way too?" There were 31 responses to this inquiry. One student's reaction to the responses was, "This item is great. Thank-you to everyone who has given us encouragement. It actually makes me feel that I will be able to handle it."

At the end of each term we asked the students to rate the worth of Confer—how useful was it, how important for their professional growth and development. Although there were some who simply did not like this mode of communication, the student responses were generally very positive on both questions. Several of those students expressed gratitude that they were able to take a computer terminal home so they could have access at their convenience. The most frequently expressed complaint during the first term was that there were too many items that were unrelated to students' specific subject area/grade. We, as mentioned previously, resolved that issue by creating sub-conferences. Another complaint was the amount of time consumed. One student expressed the dilemma in her hurriedly scrawled comment, "Confer was fun... didn't expect to get hooked but I did! Spent too much time on it though. . . and didn't get my other work done." Most students appreciated the opportunity to confer with cohorts and professionals.

As the term of student teaching and computer conferencing drew to a close, one student teacher entered a nostalgic item: "I'm going to miss this machine. I've got a lot of great memories (especially signing on around 4 a.m.) and I'm going to miss the opportunity to connect with so many people. . . Judging from the responses exhibited on Confer this term, I can't imagine the image of teachers and attitudes toward them not changing for the better."

The computer conferencing network for the directed teaching program exceeded our vision in its success, but the program was not without problems. First, there were technical difficulties with hardware. Though unable to solve all the technical problems, Media Services and the Office of Professional Development were indispensable as technical troubleshooters. Second, some of our students lived outside the area where they could gain access to the MERIT network without making long distance telephone calls. These students were hesitant to use the system and, when they did, kept their communications to a bare minimum. Third, student teachers, professional teachers, and University faculty and staff are very busy people, and it was often difficult for them to find time to participate as much as we had hoped. In fact, a comment that was frequently included on the evaluation was that there were too few participating classroom teachers and University faculty.

All things considered, however, the benefits of Confer seemed well worth the investments made by those who planned and implemented the project and by the participants. The directed teaching conferences have continued to be a success story throughout more recent terms. They have proven to be an effective way of easing the isolation felt by the student teachers and helping them maintain regular contact with their cohorts, the University faculty and staff, and professionals in the field to which they're aspiring. These conferences have also become useful tools for research.

The fact that an increasing number of students have had computer conferencing experience by the time they begin student teaching has alleviated the strain they feel at having to learn yet another new skill when they are already so overwhelmed with the challenge of learning to be a teacher. Most now look forward to the opportunity to participate in Confer, since they have become increasingly aware of the computer network as an asset to them in their preparation to be classroom teachers.

Conclusion

Computer conferencing worked at Michigan. Confer projects had broad institutional support at the University level and in the Dean's office in the School of Education. Michigan contributed not only to the professional growth of those who used Confer in these years but also to the growth of the profession itself as various uses for computer conferencing were explored.

The conferences that were the most successful in terms of our original vision were those established and used within the University community for needs that were significant to University faculty. When these needs involved practitioners, when adequate resources were made available, and when there was meaningful collaborative activity to be done, computer conferencing did indeed work as envisioned.

Conferences for consultants and professional organizations based in the public schools were successful for them but fell short of the vision of linking higher education and the field of practice. Where these consultants took the initiative to communicate with higher education faculty in public conferences or where work groups using Confer included members from both higher education and public schools, these conferences, too, were successful.

The least successful conferences were those designed as public forums for interested educators—teachers, administrators, and higher education faculty—to meet and discuss concerns of mutual interest without concrete tasks or timelines. CRLT:Micros suggests that when there is a "critical mass" of active participants, spontaneous public networking among its members can happen.

A few practitioners and graduate students who used Confer with us reported feeling shy or in awe of the professors and others who either on or off Confer expressed strong opinions and/or were known for their expert knowledge. It has been our observation, however, that when public school teachers and University faculty have used computer conferencing for discussions focused on some concrete task they are working on together, e.g., assistance to student teachers, collaborative research, or a curriculum document, the traditional cultural barrier between them tends to fall away. Once each member develops the self-concept of having a niche in the enterprise that is his/her own and that is valued, discussions engender full participation and take on a democratic tone. This may have something to do with the medium, or it may be a result of meaningful collaborative activity, regardless of the medium used for interaction.

We noticed in several school-university conferences that there seemed to be people in the group who were already cross-cultural in some way. They already had relationships that spanned these two cultures, they valued collaborative interaction, and they were in positions to do something with the ideas exchanged in such interaction. In many instances, these persons were practitioners who were also advanced graduate students or who already had working relationships with University faculty through their school districts or state professional organizations. Other times, staff persons appointed as University liaisons were effective in this role on Confer. In our experience, it was rare for members of either the University or the public school communities to interact on Confer if they were not already engaged in cross-cultural relationships formed or legitimized outside computer conferencing. Meeting on Confer did not replace face-to-face interaction.

The relative success of a conferencing experience can be characterized by the degree of fit between the multiple needs and norms of the group and its various members. Most often a good fit has much to do with the task at hand, its perceived significance to various members, and with its appropriateness for collaborative interaction. For example, in MICH:TeacherEd, student teachers had the need to talk to each other and faculty as well as to practitioners for information and moral support while they were out student teaching. Status among faculty and practitioners was naturally evened in this conference since both perspectives were important to the students. In addition, the norm during student teaching is to ask for all the help you can get.

Another facet of fit for computer conference users is the fit of conference text format and content to reading comprehension and writing skills. Skilled computer conference participants are able to read with appropriate speed and comprehension as conference text is presented by chunks that fit on a computer screen and to compose cogent responses, also with relative speed. Various populations work with content, language, and syntax that may be particular to their areas of interest. Literature teachers who look at CRLT:Micros items may find most discussion there incomprehensible. To them, it might be like reading an engineer's journal.

Another side of this issue relates to Karl Zinn's suggestion that users give some clue as to their intended tone when their text is too terse for connotative decoding by others who may otherwise misinterpret for lack of visual and/or other contextual information. Subtle aspects of this issue tend to surface during one's increasing experience with computer conferencing. How various populations create and use text that is comprehensible to their members and that fits the computer screen environment will be interesting to observe as more and more diverse populations adopt computer conferencing.

Michael Waggoner developed and managed the computer conferencing services program in the Office of Professional Development from its inception until 1988. He had advice from the outset that remained consistent in discussions with new conferencing users and organizers. For computer conferencing to work, he said that there must be:

- Something to talk about.
- Norms that support the interaction that occurs.
- Convenient access to equipment that is easy to use.
- A commitment to regular times for conference activity.

In terms of this advice, we experienced forces in the schools that worked against us, which remain unresolved. First and foremost is the matter of equipment. While computers are increasingly common in schools, modems are not. When modems are provided, the handicap that is almost always the most formidable is lack of a telephone line that can be used for computer conferencing. Often school districts have telephone systems that are difficult to use, and there is seldom access to an outside, direct telephone line except in the principal's office or the teachers' lounge.

Equally formidable for public school populations is the cost of computer conferencing. There are seldom places in current school budgets for computer conferencing time and any necessary long distance telephone charges for individual staff members. Many schools were able to use Confer by designating one or a few individuals in the district to receive computer accounts for computer conferencing at school district expense, but Confer is designed to thrive on individual participation rather than on representative contributions from organizations. Costs for computer conferencing can easily exceed amounts usually spent on professional journals by individuals, and computer conferencing is not yet seen as a low-cost substitute for face-to-face professional meetings and/or inservice workshops.

Third, since computer conferencing is outside the normal routine, it demands time that is not usually perceived as available to individuals who are busy with tasks that seem to be more directly related to their everyday work. Consultants, most often computer education consultants, were the most frequent participants from the public school community. People in these roles are accustomed to sitting at their desks reading for portions of the day. Consultants' customary telephone networking is more cumbersome than computer conferencing where participants can interact on their own schedules. Also, reading and typing text is not far beyond the scope of the traditional routines of consultants, and they are used to exchanging information, applying it to some particular context in their own setting, or routing it to some interested party's attention.

Having equipment for computer conferencing at home was sometimes an effective way to break into the routine of teachers. For these teachers, computer conferencing was related to valued job enrichment activity. However, many computer enthusiasts who earlier used home time for Confer activity eventually stopped when they became dissatisfied with how such activity expanded their work day in ways that were no longer "fun."

We can suggest another consideration for those who want to break into school routines. For teachers and building administrators, students are of high interest. When students were involved in some way, in many cases we observed telephone lines were somehow installed and people managed to get the terminal software up and running. Projects that involved only teachers and university professors talking about curriculum or professional development did not have the attention of teachers as did curriculum projects involving students, such as the MSTA's proposal that students use computer conferencing to share weather data among themselves, and the MICH:TeacherEd conferences that focused on helping student teachers.

Lastly, with regard to breaking into school routines, for administrators in public schools, general public discussion did not appear to be attractive, and keyboarding often seemed to be a source of discomfort. Administrators preferred to read, and while some administrators had secretaries enter and receive text for their review and response on paper copies, these methods did not utilize the power of computer conferencing for on-line, spontaneous dialogue among colleagues. The technology that has proliferated among administrators is the fax machine, which may be a greater fit to established office routines and communication norms.

We conclude this reflection with three factors we have found to be related to successful computer conferencing in any setting once the four conditions mentioned above are met. The first is getting appropriate technical information into the hands of group members who are computer conference novices without alienating them with computer jargon. Sometimes the conference manager or another member of the group served as a "technical assistance" person, such as we both did in several groups in which we each participated. Other times, conference participants were able to get technical assistance in language they understood from others they

knew and could talk to easily in informal hallway or telephone
conversations.

Some Confer users called the Office of Professional
Development for on-the-spot telephone help. They could also ask
for print support materials we developed to help users with Confer
as well as with a variety of hardware and software. Clancy Wolf,
the resident technical expert, also developed a Confer tutorial and
simulation with an audio tape guide for three different models of
computers. These were popular with newcomers who were initially
anxious about learning to use Confer on a public conference and/
or about the cost for computer time. Workshops to train beginners
and to train Confer organizers were also offered periodically.

Two ideas for additional support from the Office of
Professional Development were considered but not implemented.
One was a one-page newsletter that could be mailed periodically to
remind users of Confer, identify new items that might be of interest,
and provide intermediate and advanced Confer use tips. The other
was a directory of public Confer users that could be kept for their
reference both on and off line. However it is provided and from
whatever source, technical assistance and informal support available
from trusted sources on request often appeared to be critical to
conference success.

The second factor we observed across successful conferences
is that active participants develop their own traditions and routines
for conferencing. One computer coordinator told us he does his
Confer work in the evening at home after dinner. Another found it
a good way to get into the workday in the early morning. A typical
routine was to take care of what was appropriate to do on the spot,
to download and print what he wanted to think about, and to use
sticky-backed yellow paper posted on various folders, books, and
even furniture as reminders of things to do later with the information
captured. Making printed copy of selected Confer items and using
paper-pencil notes about the locations of items of interest were
usual behaviors. More advanced users who worked in Confer with
larger amounts of texts developed skills in downloading and

uploading procedures. As users matured, they gradually increased their own repertoire of skills to handle sophisticated software and more advanced Confer features such as the personal index. While we never heard that the Confer Users' Guide was extremely useful, users reported that they usually found some interesting new things to try when they went to that source for help with some specific question and skimmed through the Guide in the process.

The third factor is commitment and leadership that supports computer conferencing activity in the organizations using it. In many cases, the conference manager was the most visible facilitator once the necessary equipment was achieved and the computer accounts were opened. The amount and quality of conference activity often were perceived to be largely dependent on the frequent presence of a conference manager who provided timely, critical information as well as affective comments that pulled users into the group's camaraderie, encouraged attitudes of participation, and discouraged users from being judgmental among themselves.

Another important aspect of leadership is the commitment to computer conferencing as a medium that will be used by a group. The most success seemed to occur when the use decision was made by the organization and the necessary resources and support were provided. Where use was required and/or expected, there were hurdles to overcome, but they were minor in comparison to the hurdles encountered by groups where participation was at the discretion of autonomous individuals who were left to get their own equipment, computer accounts, and time for conferencing activity without concrete, meaningful tasks or direction.

To conclude, we have learned that while computer conferencing promotes networking that was previously not possible in education, it does not make happen what its users do not want to do anyway. What its users want to do is what proliferates. To this extent, computer conferencing is truly an empowering medium.

References

Zinn, Karl. Michigan Terminal System, UM Host. CRLT:Micros, Volume 10. Item 3, Nov. 3, 1989a.

Zinn, Karl. Michigan Terminal System, UM Host. CRLT:Micros, Volume 10. Item 10, Nov. 3, 1989b.

2

Building an Electronic Culture:
The Academical Village at Virginia

Glen Bull, Judi Harris, and David Drucker

Culture is the one thing that we cannot deliberately aim at. It is the product of a variety of more or less harmonious activities, each pursued for its own sake.
T. S. Eliot, 1949.

Thomas Jefferson used the term "academical village" to describe his design for the University of Virginia, which he founded. Student rooms were interspersed among faculty pavilions to encourage interactions among members of this community.

For several years we have been developing an electronic academical village in the Curry School of Education at the University of Virginia. This electronic village links teachers in the public schools, students in the teacher education program, and faculty at the university. The networked environment provides a community in which these groups can exchange thoughts and ideas. It not only links teachers in local schools with one another but also with teachers across the nation and in other countries.

We have established three goals in our effort to create an electronic culture. First, we wanted to provide teachers with an instructional tool for use in the classroom. A number of teachers in the surrounding public school systems have used the network in innovative and creative ways with their classes. Second, we wanted to provide teachers with a network which would allow them to communicate with one another, both for support and for exchange of educational ideas.

Finally, we wanted to include student teachers in the network so that they could participate in this educational community. Access to the electronic community complements physical visits to classrooms that occur during practica and internships. We wanted students in the teacher education program to have interactions with large numbers of teachers and viewpoints in a casual and social way that might not be possible in more formal, supervised internships. Teacher-LINK is the formal name for the component of the program designed to enhance the student teaching process by linking student teachers, university faculty, and teachers in the schools. This effort has been conducted in a joint partnership with IBM, which has contributed more than 100 microcomputers and a mainframe computer in support of the Teacher-LINK project.

Overview: Elements of an Electronic Village

Development of an electronic community is contingent upon two components. These components may be loosely described as equipment and people. In broader terms, these elements may be described as the infrastructure of hardware and software, and the underlying culture of the user community. The necessary infrastructure of hardware and software consists of microcomputers, modems, phone lines, and mail programs. The second, equally critical component is creation of an electronic culture which uses computer networks to communicate as casually and competently as the telephone is used. The second component not only requires initial training in use of the network, but also modeling of possible applications and uses.

Establishment of an electronic culture has been the responsibility of the Teacher-LINK field coordinator, Judi Harris. Installation and support of the necessary infrastructure within the school of education is the responsibility of the coordinator of the Curry School Educational Technology Center, David Drucker.

There are significant interactions among the components of infrastructure and culture. For example, an electronic mail system which is difficult to use and not easily understood by users increases the amount of training required, and also decreases the frequency with which teachers employ the system after they have learned to use it. We have employed several different electronic mail systems, conferencing systems, and news distribution networks in the Curry School, and have concluded that there are significant differences which may be expected with respect to use of various systems.

Elements of the Infrastructure

Local Hardware

An evolving mix of hardware has been used to link offices within the main education building of the Curry School. Initially, connections to the university network consisted of 1200 bits per second (bps) modems. Currently, an Ethernet serves as the backbone of a local area network (LAN) within the education building. A Novell network provides access to four 80-megabyte file servers, CD-ROM databases in the education library, networked printers in each departmental office, and other services. AppleTalk networks within the building are also linked to the Ethernet via gateways and routers. Ethernet connections provide access to other computers and services throughout the university, and at other universities. It is possible to access electronic mail on more than 150 different mainframes and minicomputers at the University of Virginia. An IBM 3090 mainframe, a CDC mainframe, and VAX, Prime, and AT&T minicomputers are some of the machines linked together. TCP/IP is the protocol which binds these computers together on a common network and allows them to communicate with one another. This environment provides a variety of electronic mail systems which can be used to examine the effect of different electronic mail interfaces. The Academic Computing Center of the University has provided extensive assistance in this area, often customizing or modifying electronic mail systems to meet specialized needs found within the public schools.

Teachers in the schools can access the network through dial-up modems at 1200 or 2400 bps.   Once the connection to the University network is established, connections to any of the mail servers on the network are possible. Other services, such as access to the University of Virginia on-line library catalog, are also available through this connection.

Extended Links: The Inter-University Networks

A variety of electronic networks link universities across the United States and other countries.   These include the ARPA Internet, BITNET, and an alphabet soup of other academic networks (Quarterman and Hoskins, 1986). For the most part these academic wide area networks (WANs) are interconnected so that a message initiated on one can be transparently routed to a recipient on another network.   In some respects these interconnections parallel telephone networks in which a long distance call may be routed across several networks in a manner that is usually transparent to the end user.   More recently gateways between the university networks and other networks such as FrEdMail (which originated in the California public schools) and commercial networks such as AppleLink have become available.

This "metanetwork" provides teachers with access not only to other teachers across town but also around the world. The classes of teachers in local school systems have communicated with other classes from Spain to Israel, as well as with teachers from Alaska to Florida in the United States. Typically, the teachers have devised instructional uses appropriate to their individual educational needs. For example, Jeanette Wells, a teacher at Walker Middle School in Charlottesville, Virginia, describes some of the uses of the network which she devised for her class:

"We have been in contact with a variety of people for a variety of reasons. All the members of my class have an Alaskan pen pal whom they write to. Also, we were in contact with a history professor from a midwestern school while we were covering a unit on American Indian history. Finally, we have contact with an instructor from another part of Virginia with whose class we do joint science experiments.

"The class was surprised to find that the Alaskan students had many interests similar to theirs (i.e., pizza, skateboarding, and 'The Cosby Show'). Students in both locations were unfamiliar with certain kinds of wildlife that their counterparts knew well (i.e., turtle, caribou). At first my students were intolerant of their pen pals' lack of knowledge, but changed their opinions once they saw that they too were unknowledgeable regarding certain things."

Jeanette integrated network interactions throughout a number of subject areas across the curriculum. For example, she incorporated letters which the class wrote to Alaskan counterparts into language arts, devised a survey for the Alaskan class in social studies, and graphed the results in a unit on charts and graphs in mathematics.

Software: Electronic Mail

The chief characteristic of electronic mail is that it is a point-to-point service which delivers an electronic message or document from one user to another user. It very much resembles its counterpart, U.S. mail, except that it is faster and generally is delivered in a matter of minutes rather than days. Electronic mail is ideal for some instructional uses, but is not as well suited for others. A significant limitation appears when an ongoing electronic conversation is conducted among a large number of people (more than a half-dozen). Since each recipient does not necessarily have the opportunity to read the replies of all the other correspondents before responding, considerable overlap and redundancy often ensues. An attempt to schedule the time and location for a luncheon meeting over a mail system typically reveals some of these limitations.

Software: Conferencing Systems and News Groups

In addition to electronic mail, a variety of other electronic
services are available on different systems. These include bulletin
boards, news distribution systems, BITNET list servers and file
servers, and conferencing systems.

A bulletin board allows a user to post items in a public forum
that can be read by all other users on the system. It serves as the
electronic equivalent of a bulletin board in a school in that respect.
At one point a bulletin board for teachers was established on one of
the University of Virginia computers to complement the electronic
mail system. However, an electronic bulletin board has several
significant limitations. The most significant is that it resides on a
single computer system. This, of necessity, implies that everyone
who uses the bulletin board must access that computer system. This
is inconvenient for teachers who may be accessing mail on a
different computer system. (At the University of Virginia it is
possible to access electronic mail on more than 150 computer
systems with a variety of mail interfaces.) It may mean that it is
necessary to log onto one system to access mail, log off, and then log
onto another system to access the bulletin board. Worse, this system
limits use to local teachers, since it is necessary for teachers in other
cities or states to call long distance to access the bulletin board.

News distribution services offer an alternative to electronic
bulletin boards. These types of services include news groups on the
USENET network, and list servers on the BITNET network. Both
of these services distribute postings to everyone who has joined the
news group (on USENET) or a list server (on BITNET). The
advantage is that it is not necessary to access the system on which
the posting originates to read it. Instead, the information is distributed across the network until it reaches each subscriber. In this
respect this system resembles a magazine distribution system,
except that electronic articles may be distributed individually as
well as by volume. In fact, refereed "electronic journals" have
begun to appear in some disciplines.

One of the limitations of both USENET news groups and BITNET list servers is that within a group postings are not organized by conversation. Some USENET readers can follow a conversational strand by using pattern matching. However, this method can only be used to follow the conversational thread if the subject line is not changed. Further, postings are not organized internally by conversational strand.

Organization by conversational strand is the approach used in one type of conferencing system, Confer, developed at the University of Michigan. Items can be posted by any user. Subsequent replies to the posted topic are appended to that item. The system displays all of the responses to a particular item before going on to the next item. We felt that this approach was so well suited to educational use that we used it for a national project involving educators (Cochran and Bull, 1988) in preference to several other systems on BITNET and USENET which might have been employed.

The Confer system met all of our expectations with respect to results and functionality. However, the telecommunications charges to access the system through Telenet were substantial, and it was not financially feasible to use the conferencing system on a widespread basis in the teacher education program. The Confer system required an operating system (the Michigan Terminal System) which was not available at the University of Virginia, so it was not possible to transport the system to Virginia to reduce telecommunication charges.

At that time a conferencing system which utilized the same structure as Confer became available for other operating systems. The Caucus conferencing system was developed by Camber-Roth, and is distributed by Metasystems, Inc. Metasystems provided a copy of the Caucus conferencing program to the Curry School, and it was incorporated into the instructional network. The Caucus conferencing system has proved to be very successful. Teachers quickly learn to use the system, and have devised a number of instructional applications that make use of the conferencing capability. Conferences have thus far been organized according to educational level and area. There are conferences for elementary students, high school students, and for teachers. Other conferences are provided for specialists in communication disorders, adaptive physical education, and members of different instructional computing classes.

Each conference must have an organizer, and the success of the conference is very dependent upon the organizer. Thus far the number of effective organizers available has limited the number of conferences which can be provided. To put it another way, there always seem to be more ideas for good conferences than there are good organizers to implement the conferences.

The version of the Caucus system that is currently being used resides on a single minicomputer just as a bulletin board does, and it is necessary to log onto that minicomputer in order to access the conferencing system. Distributed versions of Caucus and other conferencing systems have been developed, and may be available by the time that this appears in print.

Building an Electronic Culture

It is sometimes assumed that acquisition of additional equipment will provide a solution to all unmet needs. However, installation of the underlying infrastructure (hardware and software) merely provides a beginning foundation. In the long run, the cost of training and supporting users exceeds the cost of the equipment used. Failed projects in both business and education attest to the fact that networks will fail and the equipment will go unused if adequate training and user support are not provided. Equipment and training are by themselves not sufficient, however.

Activities within electronic cultures must have user-satisfying purposes in and of themselves if the culture is to thrive. The electronic academical village has served to:

-reduce feelings of professional isolation,

-provide technical assistance for infusing computer technologies into traditional curricular instruction,

-allow teachers to share local instructional resource information,

-assist in the preview and planning of student teaching internships,

-and provide emotional support for students during their first full-time teaching experience.

In the same way that physical environments, such as rain forests, country clubs, or computer-rich classrooms, have direct impact upon culture formation, so, too, do electronic "environments." The two types of computer-based communications available in the electronic academical village, electronic mail and computer conferencing, complement one another. Electronic mail extends a private messaging service to network participants by allowing them to send messages to a single addressee or small group of recipients. Computer conferencing provides a public forum for discussion, where everything that is contributed is available for perusal and response by all participants. Electronic mail can strengthen person-to-person connections; conferencing often encourages collaborative idea sharing, and therefore can help to build time-shifted and distance-independent cultures.

Electronic Environments

Within the conferencing arena, there are additional ways in which the sense of environment can be engendered. Conscious efforts toward this end are necessary, since electronic communications are decidedly non-physical, and can therefore appear to participants at first to be less "real" than face-to-face exchanges. Electronic "rooms," for example, can be created on conferencing systems into which participants can wander, such as the most popular conference in the electronic academical village, the "Lounge."

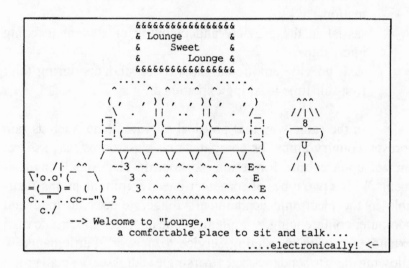

This picture greets each teacher as he or she electronically enters the Lounge. It is not surprising, then, that early item responses spoke about the "lumpy, comfortable old couch," the "coffeepot in the corner," and the "friendly faces that greet you in this place." Such cooperative fantasy-building is as much a construction of nonphysical meeting places as it is part of social interaction in nonelectronic environments.

Equally important in atmosphere-setting is the tone with which participants address one another. We have seen that conference organizers can have direct and pervasive impact upon this emotional component of the electronic milieu simply by shifting their postings into a positive, energetic demeanor.

Example of Interchange Involving
Teachers and the Conference Organizer

26:32) Linda Hutson   04-JUL-89 9:19
I also had an idea... Do you think that ALBEMARLE COUNTY and
U.Va. could or would be willing to have authors HERE??? Why
not? I know that MANY, MANY teachers would be willing to
attend. Think of what we could bring to the children after meeting
authors. Does anyone have any ideas about this or know someone
who might be interested in this at U.Va.?

- - - - -

26:33) Judi Harris   04-JUL-89 13:05
Linda, I think that that is a *great* idea, and I'll bet that Pat Crook
(the children's lit prof) might be interested in helping you with it. If
you'd like to compose a series of responses to her (anybody that's
interested) here on this item, I'll be glad to print them out and put
them in her mailbox. **Great idea!**

- - - - -

26:34) Marshall Chase   04-JUL-89 17:46
Let's get Pat Crook on here! If you need any help, I'd be glad to
lobby for Lounge :-) <smile>

Participants also communicate the tone of their text (and
most often, their positive feelings) with sideways-oriented text
pictures called "emoticons." Similar expression can be achieved
with the use of capital letters, asterisks, and exclamation points in
ways that would normally be considered excessive in other types of
written communication. Use of whimsical pictures and customized
punctuation helps to express some of the emotion that would
normally be reflected in facial affect, vocal tone, and body move-
ments that normally accompany face-to-face communication.

Computer-mediated communication is not a substitute for
face-to-face interaction. Rather, one greatly enhances the other.
Our teachers normally attend classes, hands-on workshops, or

small-group "grass-roots" sessions informally given by a peer to introduce them to use of electronic mail and conferencing. The person-to-person bonds that are forged in these sessions are often the earliest and most important means of support for new electronic inductees. In a similar way, meeting someone in person with whom a participant has been communicating only electronically strengthens the communicative bonds in ways that we suspect would be impossible otherwise. These interactions take on special significance when international electronic conversation can grow into face-to-face meetings.

Facilitating Network Interactions

Mr. Eliot's observation is cogent advice for electronic network facilitators. Without valid and user-specific reasons to use computer-mediated communication, there is no hope for the success of culture-building. We have found that facilitation is most effective when it is focused upon providing assistance with practical matters, such as:
> • learning to use the hardware and software necessary for electronic communication,
> • providing instructional resource information,
> • organizing formats of online interaction,
> • and suggesting ways in which electronic communication could be used to support teaching and learning.

This does not imply that attention should not be paid to culture-building, though. The ways in which assistance is provided—the communications opportunities created, the matching of participants with similar interests, the timing of introduction of new ideas, and the encouraging of experienced participants to take ownership of the network by assuming positions of collective responsibility for its maintenance—can and should be highly attentive to the overall goal of encouraging the development of an online community.

More than any other participant in a new network, the conference organizer is the individual upon whom much opportunity and responsibility for creating a viable online community are placed. At the inception of a new conference or network, the organizer's role as model participant is crucial. It is the organizer who is charged with setting the tone of the conference; enthusiastic, energetic, and empathetic interactive models seem to work best. It is the organizer who will post many of the original items in a conference, so it becomes important for him/her to refrain from also dominating responses to items, lest the conference have a user list of primarily one. Once active communication begins, especially in educational networks, many organizers will find themselves in managerial roles concerning both form and content. As long as policy decisions regarding appropriate conference content have been clearly made and publicly stated, organizers should feel no remorse about removing inappropriate items and responses posted to a public forum. This is not the case, of course, for private (electronic mail) communications.

It is also the organizer's job to carefully observe the social dynamics of a conference, and take precautions to plan and execute facilitative efforts according to these interaction patterns. The unstated goal of every organizer should be to eliminate as many of his/her responsibilities as possible, seeking opportunities to transfer these to other network users. This is the only way in which feelings of ownership can be permanently adopted by non-organizer participants, and this succession is the key to a lasting, thriving network. It does indeed bode well for the probable longevity of an online community when some of the once-novice participants become conference organizers.

Participation by Teacher Education Students

A five-year teacher education program was recently initiated in the Curry School. In this program, students take concurrent courses in the school of education and the college of arts and sciences. At the end of the five-year period, the students receive a bachelor's degree in their major (such as English, mathematics, etc.) and a master's degree in teaching. Educational technology is one strand which is being woven through the five-year teacher education program.

We would like every student in the teacher education program to use the computer network as a tool to facilitate their coursework prior to graduation, and to be capable of using the network as an instructional tool in their classrooms after graduation. Teacher education students are given an electronic network ID in their first course in the Curry School, EDHS 201: Teaching as a Profession. Training in use of the computer network and other subjects such as word processing is provided during an accompanying three-hour laboratory each week during the first half of the semester. Students retain their network ID as long as they are in the Curry School, and for a year after they graduate.

Faculty in the Curry School are also provided with network access. Each of the 100 faculty in the Curry School who have requested computers have been provided with one for their office. Every computer provided is also accompanied by network access. In the past this access consisted of a mix of modems and 9600 bits per second (bps) direct serial connections. The education building has now been wired with an Ethernet system which provides access to a wider range of network services.

Participation by Teachers

Every public school teacher in the two local school districts who requests an electronic ID is provided with access to electronic mail and conferencing on an unlimited time basis. Initially, micro-computers and modems provided by IBM were distributed to selected teachers in these school systems to form the nucleus of the network. Teachers and student teachers eligible for equipment were sent detailed information about the teacher network, including specific lists of how they were expected to participate (i.e., daily log-ons, peer mentoring, and attendance at 8 hours of training) if provided with an equipment set. The application process played an important role in communicating to a core group of fully-supported users the importance of active and continuous participation, helping already-overloaded teachers to place electronic communication higher on their long lists of work priorities.

Over time the initial contribution by IBM has been matched by additional equipment provided by the respective school systems. The school systems have also installed at least one phone line for telecommunications in each school building. Grants to partially defray the cost of these phone lines have been provided by the Centel Telephone Company.

For the past three years training in the use of the network and other support has been provided to public school teachers through a network facilitator funded by the Curry School. Once the network has been well established, this role will be transferred to an electronic network facilitator within each school system.

There are four assistance formats that we have found to be necessary for catalyzing and nurturing an electronic culture within public school systems.

1. Introduction to the Network

   Introduction to the network is best done in a face-to-face, hands-on format. In the electronic academical village, this takes place either peer to peer in informal settings, or in a more structured way when a group of new participants attend workshops in a networked classroom.

2. On-Line Assistance

   These initial training sessions are supplemented and extended with 24-hour electronic support from participants via the network itself.

3. Written Documentation
   Assistance is also provided by detailed and clearly-written documentation distributed in paper form at orientation sessions, some of which are also posted on the electronic network.
4. Site Visits
   Finally, site visits to local schools help to solve hardware puzzles, review aspects of electronic interaction on an individualized basis, and plan infusion of telecommunications into instructional units.

By making varied types of assistance available to networked teachers, individualized support for participants is maximized. This encourages customized and personally significant use of telecommunications facilities.

An unexpected development in the teacher network was the voluntary participation of building-level and district-level administrators. Once they realized that many of their employees were sharing job-related information via the public conferencing system, several administrators became electronic observers. These network participants often log onto the network just to read what is posted, as opposed to those who both read and respond to items. One administrator even labelled the network an "administrative window into the classroom." Similar uses have emerged for the office of teacher education at the university, especially in reference to postings by teachers and student teachers regarding internship placements.

Participation by University Faculty

Teachers in the public schools constitute the foundation of the academical village that is in the process of evolving. However, a major motivation for establishing such a community is the belief that the teacher education process will be improved if students in the school of education are able to participate in such a community. This is more likely to occur if students see their university instructors modeling the same behavior.

The motivations for use of the network by university faculty differ from those of public school teachers. University faculty have more opportunities to talk to their colleagues on both an informal and formal basis, and hence are less likely to experience feelings of isolation that may make network interactions attractive. On the other hand, they may have even more opportunities than teachers to collaborate with colleagues at other universities via wide area networks such as BITNET.

Extending the Electronic Village

Extending the Infrastructure

A number of Virginia universities, including the University of Virginia, Virginia Commonwealth University, Virginia Tech, and George Mason University, have been providing teachers in the public schools with access to their respective university mail systems. This, in turn, provides these teachers with access to the worldwide network.

These universities and the Virginia Educational Computing Association have been working with the Virginia Department of Education to develop a plan which will provide this access to all public schools in Virginia. Details for the prototype of a statewide network were developed at the 1989 annual meeting of the Virginia Educational Computing Association (Bull, Harris, Lloyd, and Short, 1989). Several principles were agreed upon at that meeting.

1. The public school network should be compatible with the existing university network system.
2. The network should be based on a distributed computing system.

3. The user interface for the electronic mail system should
   be simple to use.
4. All school districts in Virginia should share a common
   mail interface.

This model will place a microcomputer which will function as a
local mail server in each school district. Teachers will be able to
make a local phone call to access the mail server. Local school
district mail servers will in turn transmit the data to university nodes.
This model is known as a distributed computing network, in contrast
to a centralized model in which users directly access a single
centrally-located computing facility. We believe that distributed
computing represents the architecture which will underpin effective
electronic cultures of the future. Virginia's Department of Education has been chartered to establish a statewide communications
network through its Strategic Plan for 1988-1994. Implementation
of this plan will result in a single seamless educational network in
Virginia which will link all educational levels from kindergarten
through doctoral programs.

Extending the Culture

The first instinct of an administrator or instructional tech-
nologist may be to hierarchically structure a new electronic network
from the top down, beginning with university and school administrators. We have found that some modifications to that idea increase
the impact and make for more fertile network growth. Certainly
administrative approval (especially when it directly impacts upon
funding) is a prerequisite to the germination of a new electronic
culture. We have found that once administrative approval is
secured, a grass-roots approach to attracting participants is most
effective. Instead of requiring all high school science teachers to
join the network, we have found that soliciting volunteers in the
manner described previously establishes a more solid foundation.
The best publicity for expanding a teacher network is presented

informally and in an unsolicited format by excited networked teachers. And, not surprisingly, presenting administrators with evidence of exciting telecommunications projects that are already occurring in their schools' classrooms is far more convincing evidence for increased funding than even the most carefully conceived master plan.

These grass-roots methods can also be applied to the formation of teacher networks in previously unconnected geographic areas. Once again the lesson of active user base is important to remember. If a new network is conceived as a new node to an existing, ever-expanding international network, new users have convincing reason to participate. Experienced users are available to support and encourage fledgling efforts, and relevant information exists to be shared. Adding new users to existing groups of experienced users in this fashion increases the probability of a "variety of more or less harmonious activities, each pursued for its own sake" that Eliot described.

References

Bull, G., Harris, J., Lloyd, J., and Short, J. (1989). The electronic academical village. *Journal of Teacher Education*, *40* (4), 27-31.

Cochran, P., and Bull, G. (1988). Electronic conferencing. *Journal for Computer Users in Speech and Hearing*, *4* (1), 6-13.

Eliot, T.S. (1949). *Notes towards the definition of culture*. San Diego, CA: Harcourt Brace Jovanovich.

Quarterman, J. S., and Hoskins, J. C. (1986). Notable computer networks. *Communications of the ACM*, *29* (10), 932-971.

3

Grassroots Networking on Big Sky Telegraph: Empowering Montana's One-Room Rural Schools

Frank Odasz

Financial pressures and demographic trends continue to threaten rural Montana schools with closure or consolidation. Telecommunication literacy increasingly appears to be a viable means by which rural communities can succeed in rural economic development. Dwindling financial resources for many community services mandate better use of information technology for the survival of our rural communities and cherished rural lifestyle.

The Big Sky Telegraph's mission statement is: "To empower rural residents through the sharing of knowledge access skills among rural teachers." This goal builds on the fact that rural teachers have long served the role of information specialists in rural communities.

The original objective of the Big Sky Telegraph project was to link 114 one-room schools in Montana through a multi-line microcomputer network for peer information sharing and the distribution of resources to rural schools. This objective was implemented by providing modems to rural schools, teaching how to use them economically, and developing resources for efficient circulation among the schools. Currently, Big Sky Telegraph offers electronic mail, conferencing, educational databases, library access services, user-maintained information menus, online telecommunications classes, and an educational software preview loan library (coordinated by electronic mail.)

Project Beginnings

US West and the M. J. Murdock Charitable Trust provided
$106,000 to the Western Montana College Foundation for the
project. A high speed and capacity microcomputer with seven
modems for seven phonelines was purchased. The operating
system for our system was Xenix, a Unix variation produced by
Santa Cruz Operations, Inc. Foxbase was the database software
(dbIII compatible), and a carefully customized Xbbs conferencing
software provided our unique, easily teachable conferencing system.
The cost for the software and hardware was $15,000 for a system
capable of expanding to thirty-two phonelines and handling thousands of regular users.

Two quarter-time staff were in charge of the project: a
director/system operator/instructor and a resource coordinator.
Technical support and custom programming were provided by
consultant remotely by modem from Colorado Springs. Other part-
time help was added as usage grew.

Big Sky Telegraph went online January 1, 1988. Over the
first year and a half, 17,000 calls were made to the system, 10,000
messages left by some 500 persons. Over one hundred schools have
been online in some capacity with 150 individuals being regular
users of the system.

Ten objective-based lessons, received over a five-week
period, consisted of the mastery learning online class format. A
class packet with software instructions, a syllabus, and the first three
lessons was sent to each teacher. All instruction was received at the
teacher's location, at any time convenient. By the third lesson the
teachers learned to "capture" or download the remaining lessons
directly from the Telegraph system. A high degree of interaction
was possible between teacher and student through online messaging.

The online class focused on the generic online skills necessary to call any of the 13,000 bulletin board systems nationally. Calls to other online systems were a requirement of the class. Library resource requests and participation in a software preview loan library were also required.

Two 800 numbers provided ten hours of free connect time per rural teacher during the five-week online class. Teachers were expected to pay their own phone costs after completing the class.

- Ten hours at $16/hr (prime time rate) equals........ $160
- The one credit class charge per teacher is..............$ 75
- The cost of the modem was....................................$129
  Total cost per community/rural school....................$364

Each teacher who volunteered to take the one credit online class was given a modem to use with the school's existing microcomputer. Prometheus 1200A Internal Promodems were used at a cost of $129 for both modem and telecommunications software. The total cost for providing this one credit class was $364.

During the first year and a half, seventy teachers completed the online class. Several had never used a computer before, even though there was one in the classroom. Voice calls were used to offer encouragement and work out complex questions or problems. Some teachers needed their confidence boosted regularly; others worked through all ten lessons with barely a question.

Two thirds of the rural schools invited to participate in the project had microcomputers. About one third of these rural teachers expressed immediate interest in the class. Computer fear was an obvious inhibitor as was the time available beyond the teaching duties. The mastery learning format of the inservice training course, and the need for recertification credits, were prime motivators, along with the promise of easy and continuing access to educational resources and to other rural teachers.

Interactive computer conferencing between teacher and student, and among students in a public or private message format, was used initially in a question/answer format. Students learned that if they could articulate a specific question, a quality answer would be there the next time they called. For instance, when stuck on how to save online information to a data disk the teacher would list the steps attempted and the results. The instructor could then identify the missing or incorrect step in any sequence of procedures and get the teacher going again.

System Benefits

Messaging among students and requests for resources from various resource providers were required class objectives. Public postings of resource needs and teaching tips were encouraged. Anyone could send a message, any time, from anywhere.

The biggest problem with teaching online skills is that the online medium of communication is significantly different from voice calls or the postal service. The implication of being able to communicate with anyone in the world, any time, for any reason, from the keyboard in a rural school, can be overwhelming.

Minimizing the amount of time required to communicate with given individuals effectively allows regular communications with a larger number of people than with other media. This "superconnectivity" is but one example of the numerous subtle advantages of the medium often not immediately clear to newcomers.

Telephone tag effectively prohibits up to 50% of the phone calls between busy persons from being connected, versus 100% completed through electronic mail. Time lost to polite socializing is minimized as well, creating potential time efficiencies.

Being "online" is an experience first and foremost. There is no substitute for first hand experience. Most people do not really understand the advantages the media offers until they actually send and receive messages by themselves. Even then they only begin to understand the vast potential of their new resource.

We found four identifiable stages to learning online skills: uncertainty, insight, internalization, and enlightened expectations. At the first stage the teachers often experience doubt as to whether they will be able to master the basic computer skills. A very shallow understanding of the potential benefits is common at this stage, though there is the general impression that there are advantages. For the individual at the "uncertainty" stage, it is important to keep the instructional tasks very simple with a mastery learning format. Easily obtainable objectives are necessary to build confidence, as well as encouraging messages whenever possible. "Technofear" and related ego-protecting excuses are strongest at this stage.

Often a teacher will take many months to warm up to the idea of going online, as if preparing subliminally for a major change in behavior. It is important for the teacher to feel in control and not forced to learn online skills. Once proving that the teacher can communicate with peers online, there is a surge of optimism.

At this "insight" phase the teacher accepts that telecommunications skills are not beyond reach and begins to see an increasing number of ways to benefit. Promises of regular use are common. Often this is a plateau of learning and some teachers find their old habits pull them away from incorporating online skills into their daily routines. "I don't have the time" is a frequent excuse which shows that the timesaving advantages of communication online are not yet clearly understood. The fact that better resource access will save class preparation time for the teacher has not been fully grasped.

The "internalization" stage is when, through regular use, the teacher begins to view the online skills as merely an extension of one's self and the teaching role. At this point "being online" is little more than making a voice telephone call. Usage falls into a pattern of purposeful use. This is a subtle, yet crucial step: when the external promises of telecommunications become part of one's internal reality.

After a teacher internalizes the online experience and becomes a regular, even casual user, there is an acceptance that this medium has even greater potential benefits, which leads to the fourth stage, "enlightened expectations." Now the real potential starts to percolate deep down in the teacher's consciousness and serious questions as to what else is possible begin to arise.

At this stage the teacher begins to make an internal commitment to fully pursue the potential of the online mode. This may be a year or more after initially going online. Willingness to serve as an online resource person, to tutor others online, or even to create and teach classes online for other teachers, is common at this point.

The need for initial person-to-person contact, whether face-to-face, through voice telephone calls, or through electronic mail, cannot be overemphasized. Group and peer teaching opportunities are encouraged when a high degree of anxiety is present. Self-motivated teachers require only access to the lessons.

Bearing in mind the considerable conceptual growth involved in these stages, a teacher's initial online experiences must result in an immediate tangible benefit to warrant future calls. Our response to this need was to post a list of quality copyrighted software online and instruct the teacher to request three software packages in a message. The selected software packages are then sent to the teacher for a two-week loan period. $10,000 was spent on a quality educational software preview loan library to initially attract the teachers and to demonstrate the efficient distribution of resources, using electronic mail, to resource-poor rural schools. Messages were used to conveniently inform a teacher which school requires the resources next, effectively keeping them in rotation among the schools throughout the semester while minimizing the costs of returning them to Western Montana College for remailing. Science kits, instructional videos, holiday plays, and other resources were quickly added to the resource distribution program.

Many formerly computer illiterate teachers demonstrated avid enthusiasm after reviewing quality software. We were surprised to find that our software loan library served as an effective, economical, ongoing form of painless instructional computing inservice training.

School boards typically feared phone costs would grow out of control, despite assurances that $5/week would be the ongoing phone cost. One twenty-minute phone call at $16/hr prime time rates costs roughly $5. If messages and text are captured quickly for offline reading, and long messages are written offline for later transfer at four pages per minute, up to 80 pages of text can be exchanged during one twenty-minute session. The usefulness of this information becomes the issue and the major focus of the Telegraph's function. Teacher submissions are encouraged. In contrast, school boards did not flinch in regard to mailing costs since they seemed to be more controllable than use of the telephone.

As a rule, school boards understood the potential of being "online" only after the teachers demonstrated the system as part of their online class. Most people do not understand online communications simply by hearing about it. Firsthand experience is very important before the awareness takes place. The typical response to a live demonstration was enthusiasm by school board members, often resulting in the purchase of printers or extra disk drives to support the teacher's online efforts.

Access and Cost

Big Sky Telegraph's motto is "By educators, for educators." An open access policy defines it as a true public system. No one is turned away. A $10/$15/$20 sponsorship fee for educators, community service organizations, and business offices, respectively, includes participation in the resource distribution programs and specific advanced features such as advanced conferences and global messaging.

Ongoing costs to a school would be:

• $5/week phone charges times four weeks/month......$20
• $10/month sponsorship charge................................$10

Total monthly costs per school....................................$30

Thirty dollars per month is the total cost for all services per school, not counting mailing costs. For a ten month school year that would be $300 per school per year. Many schools need a year's lead time to work this into school budgets, so the initial response to the sponsorship option was low, but it picked up over time.

System Problems

The biggest problems were primarily technical, concerning the correct hardware and software settings of the modems, printers, and telecommunications software. We recommend sending the modem and telecommunications software preconfigured for the teacher's specific computer and printer type. Getting access to a phoneline is not as big a problem in one-room schools as it is in larger schools, since most one-room schools have a phone available.

Those teachers without wordprocessing experience had a more difficult time conceptualizing their use of the computer for communications due to their struggling with such basics of using a computer as how to save files on a floppy disk.

Noisy phone lines cause alien characters to appear on the computer screen, often causing concern to the teachers. Ignoring the "extra" characters or calling back and hoping for a cleaner line were the only solutions. In extreme cases of line noise teachers would be unable to connect at a transmission speed of 1200 baud and would have to drop down to 300 baud. Line noise prohibited some schools from use of the system, while others became discouraged. Line noise tends to come and go, depending on weather and anomalies in the phone system. About 20% of the teachers reported noise problems sufficient to affect their use of the system.

Teachers having completed the online class are often called on to demonstrate their skills to the local community or to help other teachers in the region get online. The online class emphasizes the role of community information specialist with the teacher serving as a link between the rural community and statewide resource persons.

Rural teachers are the logical contact persons for such a rural community outreach project. Historically, the rural teacher has been the information hub of a rural community. Rural teachers from resource poor schools understand the need for better informational resources and have shown great patience and perseverance in learning how to access information. Rural teachers tend to be self-starters and, perhaps out of necessity, have had to be more resourceful than other teachers. The success of Big Sky Telegraph is very much to be credited to the patience and perseverance of these pioneers of rural America's educational frontier.

Common quotes from rural teachers beginning the class include: "I must look really stupid, but don't give up on me!" and "I'm old and I'm slow, but I'm going to learn this!" Those who did stick with the course, without exception, succeeded. Patience and perseverance are the keys to learning in our increasingly technological and rapidly changing world.

Spread of Use

As word got around about the efficiencies of online communications, and that a hundred communities were "online" through the local rural schools, other groups expressed interest in getting online. Our strategy was to vend excess communications services to interested individuals and organizations as part of our effort to become economically self-sufficient while broadening our base of resource providers.

A generic problem in rural communities, both for business and education, is that no comprehensive listings of available services, resources, and expertise are available. Telegraph provides these listings and the efficient means for matching needs and services in a format operated by the grassroots individuals themselves.

An online system which allows organizations to share information with rural schools and communities can easily be used to develop grant proposals. Numerous organizations have been able to easily find funding for projects that involve the use of telecommunications to disseminate information to an established base of over a hundred communities.

Small grants have been awarded for online instruction to the Anaconda Job Corps, the Women's Center of Dillon, and the Women's Economic Development Group Organization (WEDGO) of Missoula. In addition, the twelve women's centers of Montana received funding to learn microcomputer telecommunications to empower their efforts.

The Headwaters Resource, Development, and Conservation Organization is a grassroots leadership group presently linking offices from rural towns in seven Southwest Montana counties through Telegraph. Recently they received a grant for an online Agricultural Incubator Without Walls to serve the same seven counties. A fulltime director/circuit rider was hired and supplied with a laptop microcomputer for "on-the-road/on-line" communications.

Several disabled individuals are collecting information on use of telecommunications and technology for gainful employment in the "ReAbled" conference. Trained and ready to train others online, these individuals have started to look for funding to broadly share their newfound skills. A "Work-at-Home" conference has been created to collect and disseminate the rapidly growing body of information on using microcomputers and telecommunications to work out of the home.

Western Montana College's rural education center received a large grant to promote drug education in rural schools. Telegraph will be used to help share this information.

Western's graduates will use telecommunications to communicate with faculty and campus resource persons during their first year teaching, and undoubtedly beyond. One quarter of Western's faculty is currently online, actively serving as resource persons at their convenience.

English 101 was taught "online" to advanced students from the local high school as well as to students at Western. More and better student writing was produced than in a normal face-to-face English class. Students learned communicative writing by using the medium to "talk" with both the teacher and other students. Students used aliases to allow nonsocially biased evaluations of each other's writings.

Using reading and writing, interactively, involves students more integrally in the content of the class. Students must participate and interact as part of the instruction; no one can just "sit" passively in the back of the room, as in a normal classroom. There are subtle but clear advantages to an online class. More interactivity between student and teacher occurs than in a face-to-face class. The interaction tends to be more mind-to-mind and less socially oriented. An online class requires more organizational and interactive effort on the part of the teacher and self-motivation and self-discipline on the part of the students.

A library media specialist for the Office of Public Instruction at the State Capitol created and taught a one credit class to individuals statewide entitled "Information Access Skills for Rural Educators." Two master teachers, one in science and one in home economics, are planning to create and teach online classes.

A grant for $5,000 was received by Western from the Intermountain Community Library and Information Services (ICLIS) project to create an online version of "Computer Literacy for the

IBM," to be offered through community libraries in four states: Montana, Wyoming, Colorado, and Utah.

The Montana State Library is bringing five departments online, the Special Education Co-ops of Dillon and Deer Lodge are online, and the Forest Service is represented by Smokey Bear, who leaves penpal messages for rural students.

Individuals and organizations have the option of creating their own information menus and updating them remotely. Computer supplies and desktop publishing services are available from individuals who post their business services in this manner.

Evaluation of Use

As non-educator use grew, a completely separate bulletin board system was created to be run on the same hardware. Presently we have two systems working in partnership: one for educators and librarians and one for rural economic development and agricultural and community services. Big Sky Telegraph can continue to clone itself as the need dictates.

Functioning as an online co-op, Big Sky Telegraph effectively provides individuals and organizations with an economical means to benefit from microcomputer telecommunications.

Our choice of a supermicro over a mini or mainframe computer is one important reason why Telegraph has succeeded. To avoid compatibility problems and to have the largest amount of quality software tools available for system design, we chose a 386 microcomputer. Any micro with a modem can connect with the system and the online databases. This is often not as easily achieved on larger systems.

It is no small point that Big Sky Telegraph is staffed with two quarter time persons with no formal computer science training. However, Telegraph's staff did have writing skills, interpersonal skills, and considerable microcomputer experience. A fulltime, dataprocessing professional was not required, although such a consultant is on retainer.

Many educational online efforts have failed because the needs of teachers were not straightforwardly addressed in a user-friendly manner. A common mistake is to assume teachers will be enthusiastic about the potential and will overlook the details of the technical interface. Even a couple of unnecessary technical steps can mean a significant number of teachers will find a given procedure too tedious to attempt again.

Like other public and quasi-governmental activities, it was anticipated that Telegraph might be hindered by the institutional politics and turf battles that can occur. Another major reason for Telegraph's success is that a bottom-up approach, working directly with the rural teachers, allowed the project to grow. The system was operating successfully before it had political exposure.

A common misperception is that because "information is power," ownership of an online system will translate to political power. Unless the intent is to restrict access to information, the "power" is in the use of the medium, not in ownership of the hardware. Greater connectivity is not a given through ownership; it comes though direct use of the advantages of the medium.

Possibly because "technofear" is occasionally high among administrators, they repeatedly proved the least likely to show interest in communicating online. Telecommunications literacy among administrators is a problem, because without direct experience, one usually does not understand the online mode of communication well enough to foster its use.

The role of the system operator (sysop) is one of supportive instructor, who initiates communications with dozens of persons on a regular basis. Involving persons integrally in the use of the system is a subtle role. Sharing the sense of ownership of the system with others is paramount. Creating a sense of purpose and community, the sysop awards the roles of online tutor, community information specialist, resource person, and statewide expert to as many as possible.

Dozens of statewide resource persons are formally listed with their specialty, ready to answer questions from anyone. A trained rural teacher has only to pass on information requests from community members and retrieve responses, to function effectively as a community information specialist.

Big Sky Telegraph is a virtual community, defined by common interests in educational sharing and community development, not by physical location. Like-minded persons are invited to call Big Sky Telegraph via modem at 406-683-7680 (parameters 1200 baud, 8N1.) Type "bbs" at the login for the Rural Teachers Network or "hrn" for the Headwaters Regional Network, covering rural economic development and community services.

4

Computer Conferencing and
Mass Distance Education

Anthony R. Kaye

This chapter briefly reviews the first large-scale use of computer-mediated communication (CMC), including computer conferencing and electronic mail, in an adjunct mode in a multimedia distance education course with large numbers of students. The course in question is a 400-hour second year undergraduate course at the British Open University, with annual enrollments of around 1500 students, and involving 70 part-time tutors. The course is a multi-disciplinary one, covering the social and technological aspects of the use of new information technologies.

The first part of this chapter outlines the rationale for introducing CMC into the distance education situation, specifically in terms of the use of the medium for regular updating of a course, and for increasing the opportunities for interaction among and between students, tutors, and course developers. It then goes on to describe the Open University's growing electronic campus, a virtual environment where central and regional university staff, tutors, students, alumni, and other members of the university's dispersed community can meet, socialize, collaborate, and learn from each other. The second part of this chapter looks at the effects and implications of the use of computer conferencing within an Open University course, with specific reference to the roles of the course team, the tutors, and the students. In particular, it asks to what extent CMC as a medium can empower students and tutors in the distance learning environment—namely, give them a stronger role in the educational process, and an enhanced opportunity to contribute and share their own knowledge and experience as adult learners.

Old and New Media in Distance Education

Distance education systems, which provide instruction to large numbers of students spread over wide geographical areas, characteristically use a range of different media and teaching methods, each associated with particular learning goals. For example, specially written print materials, designed to encourage active participation by the reader, and to allow a variety of reading strategies, are generally used to convey the principal academic content of a course. Television broadcasts may be used to demonstrate scientific experiments, to visualize dynamic processes, or to convey primary source materials of a visual nature, whereas live radio broadcasts often serve feedback and magazine functions. Contact with tutors and other students, at face-to-face meetings or over the telephone, is generally the occasion for discussing learning difficulties related to particular concepts in the course, for analyzing homework assignments, or for carrying out group learning activities. Correspondence tuition provided by tutors to individual students is usually focused on assignment work submitted for grading purposes. Other media traditionally used in the distance education context (e.g., audiocassettes, videocassettes, CAI software) each have their specific role to play in what is generally a carefully orchestrated educational composition.

A major drawback to many distance education programs is the relatively "inert" nature of the course— especially when these consist of expensively produced integrated multi-media materials (e.g., videotapes, texts, CAI software, broadcasts, etc.). Updating and changing of such courses in the light of new research and perspectives are costly, and indeed many distance education courses are designed to be re-run over periods of 6 -10 years in essentially their original form, thus amortizing high course development costs over an extended period of time. The changes that an individual classroom teacher might make in response to student needs and new developments in the field become impossible in a standard distance education course. Another problem common to traditional distance education is the lack of opportunity for dialogue, debate, conversational learning, and collaborative work. Much emphasis is thus placed on the personal motivation and self-reliance of the individual student, who lacks the many occasions for interactive discussion, argument, and group activity that characterize any good face-to-face educational situation involving mature adult learners. Furthermore, tutors are often employed primarily as mediators of the packaged course materials, and as evaluators of an individual student's work, rather than as facilitators of group-based learning processes.

It could be argued that the new information technologies which involve selective interactivity (giving learners access to computer-based and easily updated sources of information) and full interactivity (communication with other learners and with tutors) will help remedy these drawbacks (Henri, 1988), and give students and tutors a more central role in the educational process. *A priori*, it would seem that the increasingly widespread computer-based communications media should be able to bring a new, interactive, convivial, and collaborative dimension into the traditionally very individual, even solitary, distance learning experience (see, for example, Lamy, 1985).

Asynchronous computer-based messaging and other forms of computer-mediated communication could, theoretically, play a major role in enhancing the quality of distance education, precisely by empowering the students and tutors, and giving them a more active and participatory role in the educational process. Evidence from trials of computer conferencing within a traditional teacher-centered educational paradigm (the "virtual classroom," the "online graduate seminar") suggests that students and teachers can replicate electronically the dialogue that occurs in the face-to-face class, and that in some respects (e.g., increased levels of turn-taking by students) this electronic dialogue may be even richer (Hiltz, 1986; Harasim, 1987). Thus it should be possible to use computer conferencing in conjunction with other, more traditional, distance education media, to give a stronger voice to students and tutors in distance education programs.

Features of computer-mediated communication (CMC) which seem particularly adapted to the distance education situation include:

> • the overcoming of space, time, and access constraints to communication among students and tutors: any one user can conveniently find and contact any other users of the network, in a way which is virtually impossible using traditional communication methods;
> • the convenience of a store and collect technology for message handling: texts can be sent and read at times chosen by each individual user;
> • the text-based nature of the medium (as opposed to voice or audiovisual communication), which is consonant with the skills of textual analysis and composition, which are key features of the distance learner's repertoire;
> • the central storage of all text, so that messages or parts of messages can be retrieved at will at a later date, and used in a variety of ways (e.g., text can be down-loaded and edited into other documents, written comments from fellow-students or a tutor can be incorporated into an ongoing piece of work, the text of a conference can be subsequently edited to produce a report);
> • the facility for group communication, which could be used for self-help activities among students, for co-operative learning, for on-line seminars, and for team-work in creation of project documents and assignments.

This chapter attempts to present an initial analysis of the effects of providing computer conferencing technology to over 1000 students and 70 tutors in a multi-media distance education course at the Open University in Britain. It examines, specifically, the extent to which the inclusion of an "electronic campus" in a mass audience distance education course can be said to "empower" the students and tutors, and the ways in which the use of computer communications technology has modified the relationship among course developers, students, and tutors.

The Open University's "Electronic Campus"

When the Open University decided to proceed with a major implementation of a computer-mediated communication system for one of its high population undergraduate courses, a review of available software led to the choice of the CoSy conferencing system, developed at the University of Guelph in Ontario. CoSy thus forms the basis of the University's national "electronic campus."

The CoSy Conferencing System

The operation of CoSy can be explained from the user's point of view through the metaphor of the writer's desk (see Figure 1). This metaphor is particularly appropriate to the distance learner's situation. It emphasizes CMC as a medium of written discourse (correspondence has always been the lifeblood of distance learning), but it also shows the different types of written communication that are possible, and hints at how the central computer stores and structures information pertaining to users and to conferences, thus promoting a far more active and extensive form of communication than traditional correspondence.

The Main Features of the CoSy System Include:

- electronic mail, with separate "baskets" for different categories of mail (new mail, held mail, acknowledged mail);
- conferences, which can be "read only" (i.e., essentially for posting notices) or "read/write" (for collaborative discussion), open or closed, confidential (i.e., unlisted) or

public (details appear in a public conference directory); a given conference may have several "topics," each one set up by the conference moderator; messages in conferences can be searched in various ways, and the system provides information on the status of each conference (numbers of read and unread messages, date and time when each member last accessed the conference, etc.);

• "conversations," which are single topic group discussion areas designed for informal communication—any user can set up a conversation, and any member of a conversation can join any other member of CoSy to it; conversations are not publicly listed, do not have moderators, and the messages auto-destruct when the last member resigns;

• a "scratchpad" area for preparing and editing message texts on-line, although the use of PC's and local editors means that many users prepare their contributions off-line, before connecting to the system and uploading them;

• directories of users, containing their personal résumés, and of conferences.

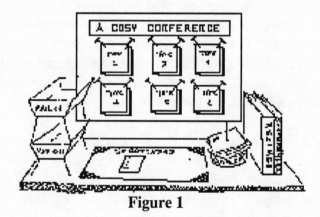

Figure 1

The "Writer's" Desk

The Open University's National Computer Network

CoSy runs on the Academic Computing Service's VAX cluster at Milton Keynes, where the University's academic and administrative headquarters are based, and is accessible from anywhere in the country. The Open University is a national institution, catering to over 100,000 home-based adult students throughout Britain. Local support (e.g., tuition, counseling) for students is organized through 13 Regional Centers and 3 sub-offices throughout the country. Each of these sites houses dial-up multiplexor nodes which are connected to the VAX cluster in Milton Keynes via leased lines. Staff in the regional centers can use terminals or PC's from their offices to connect to the VAX cluster. Students and part-time tutors throughout the country who have ID's on the system can telephone their nearest dial-up node and be connected through to CoSy, paying only the cost of the phone call to that node. Unfortunately, students living outside the local dial-up range of a node pay long-distance telephone charges—they are in fact doubly disadvantaged, as they also tend to have to travel farthest to study centers for face-to-face tutorials.

The First Inhabitants of the Electronic Campus

The CoSy system was installed at the Open University primarily for use in the second-year undergraduate course, an Introduction to Information Technology: Social and Technological Issues [course code DT200]. This is one of over 120 undergraduate courses, and the only one currently using computer communication on any scale. It is a popular course, with annual enrollments of around 1500 students. The course was first offered in 1988, and is now entering its fourth year of presentation. It is a standard multimedia OU course in many respects, with print, audio-visual, and face-to-face components. However, about 25% of the student's estimated 400 hours' study time is spent on practical work activities, using a PC at home. These activities include learning to use word-processing, communications, and spreadsheet and data-base software, as well as an approximate 10 hours connect time throughout the year on CoSy.

CoSy is presented to the students taking DT200 as providing an "electronic campus" (see Figure 2) where they can go to the "Mail Building" to collect and send their mail, socialize with other students in the "conversation area," and take part in formal on-line tutorials (in local tutor group and regional conferences) in the "Tutorial Building." Other buildings on this virtual campus include a "Training Center" (where students can learn how to use CoSy), a "Student Union" with a forum conference to which all students, tutors, and course team members can contribute, and an "Information

Figure 2
Electronic Campus "Map"

Center" where urgent notices from the course team are posted in a "news" conference.

There is also a Records Office, where students can look up other CoSy users' résumés, and scan the list of public conferences. Not shown on the map is a senior common room, which is a restricted, unlisted conference open only to tutors and course team members. This is the place where tutors provide feedback to the course team, make proposals for improvements to the course, and discuss assessment issues. Current students also have the chance to get in touch with, and obtain advice and guidance from, DT200 "alumni," who took the course in previous years, and who have asked to be able to keep their ID's on CoSy. This type of peer teaching and help is not normally possible on conventional OU courses.

The top left-hand end of the campus map indicates that students on DT200 can, if they wish, spend time in reading and contributing to other (non course) conferences on CoSy, as the early residents of the campus include a small number of central and regional staff who have taken up this new medium with enthusiasm. In mid-1989, there were around 100 open conferences on CoSy, on topics ranging from the USSR and China to film reviews, writing in French, the latest Macintosh software, and the quality of life in Milton Keynes. There is even a collectively authored spy novel which is now several hundred pages long. A small but growing number of overseas campus personalities (including students living abroad, and academics and researchers from France, the USA, Canada, Denmark, Australia, and the USSR) bring an international dimension to the growing electronic community.

Altogether, at the present time, there are over 450 group conferences and conversations on the OU's CoSy system, about half of which are currently active. The total numbers of messages in these conferences and conversations exceed 29,000, while nearly 100,000 email messages have been written since CoSy became operational in 1987.

It is not the intention to present here a systematic evaluation of computer conferencing at the Open University, and, in any case, it is too early yet to make any conclusive judgments. The use of CoSy by students and tutors on the DT200 course in its first year of presentation is analyzed by Mason (1989a). She concludes by saying that: "...for the majority of students, tutors, and course team members, computer conferencing was an interesting but marginal activity. For the committed or 'converted' minority, however, there is little doubt that this medium was an exciting, innovative, and satisfying way of participating in distance teaching and learning."

The remainder of this chapter reviews some of the effects of the introduction of the CoSy conferencing system on the three major constituencies involved in an Open University course: namely the course team, the tutors, and finally, and most importantly—the students. This review is based on the experience with the course DT200, already mentioned above.

The Course Team

Open University courses are developed and produced by course teams made up of academic specialists from the appropriate faculties, external consultants and assessors, radio and television producers, educational technologists, and editors. Responsibility for the overall direction of the team's work is invested in a course chair, generally one of the full-time central faculty staff, and day-to-day scheduling and organization are carried out by a course manager. One or more regionally-based staff tutors on the team will generally play a key role in developing ideas for tutorial support and for the recruitment and training of the part-time tutors who will be responsible for grading students' work and for running tutorials once the course has started.

The activities of a course team can be divided into two major phases—course production and course presentation. The course production phase may last up to three years, and is the period during which the course develops from an initial outline to a completed package of print, audio-visual material, and software, at a production cost of the equivalent of about 1 million US$ per course. (1) The considerable scale and cost of the course production operation at the Open University only hints, of course, at the intellectual challenge and conceptual complexity of developing the academic structure and content of a multi-disciplinary course which attempts to bring together a treatment of the social, technological, and practical issues underlying the use and understanding of new information technologies. The DT200 production course team included among its members sociologists, economists, psychologists, educational researchers, and academic experts in computing, electronics, and telecommunications. It was no small achievement to obtain consensus on the main themes of the course and the ways in which they should be treated, despite regular fortnightly and monthly team meetings over a two-year period.

Once the materials for an Open University course have been produced, the original course team is disbanded, and a small "maintenance" team is established for the 5-8 year period over which the course is presented. Each year during this course life, a new cohort of students studies the course, and course tutors take responsibility for tutorials and for evaluation of students' homework assignments. Each tutor is responsible for 20-25 students, and most tutors will stay with a course, helping a different group of students in their locality each year.

The normal responsibilities of the maintenance course team include:

- •making minor changes and improvements to the course structure and materials each year, based on feedback from students and tutors;
- •re-writing the assignment and examination materials each year;
- •monitoring tutors' marking of assignments; and

organizing the marking of end-of-year examination papers.

How has the introduction of computer conferencing changed the ways in which the course team works? *A priori*, one would have thought that the DT200 production course team would have been an ideal candidate for the use of computer conferencing for administrative purposes, and for progressing decisions and discussion of drafts of course materials in between the regular face-to-face meetings of the team. After all, the team had taken a collective decision to include computer conferencing as an integral part of the course for students and tutors, most members of the team used word-processing software for writing drafts of their material, and modems, communications software, technical backup, and reimbursement of connect charges for home-based users were all available. Furthermore, it often proved difficult to organize face-to-face meetings of course sub-groups at times that were convenient to all members: many of the full-time faculty were involved in other academic and administrative duties, and some of the team contributors were external consultants. So all the necessary conditions for effective use of computer conferencing for academic collaboration and administration seemed to be reunited in the team (2).

However, the fact is that only a few members of the team used CoSy at all during the course production phase, and this use was mainly restricted to online discussions of the future role of CMC in the course, by a small number of proponents of this technology on the team. With the benefit of hindsight, it is easy to list the reasons why CMC was not used significantly during the course production phase as a working tool, even though special conferences were set up on CoSy to discuss different parts and blocks of the course:

> • during the production period (essentially 1986 and 1987) both the campus network and the national dial-up network were being upgraded, and very few academic staff on the course team had developed the habit of using even electronic mail, let alone conferencing, as working tools;

• it would have been very difficult to have gotten all the members of the course team using CoSy on a regular basis during this period, hence any items posted onto the different block working conferences on CoSy, or any material sent to team members via email, had to be duplicated via the traditional channels of paper memos and face-to-face meetings;

• pressure on staff to complete their contributions on schedule was particularly severe, given the complexity of the course and its inter-disciplinary nature; as a result, many course team members felt they did not have time to learn how to use CMC (and were probably not convinced that, having learned to use it, it would save them time!);

• many course team members may well have been skeptical about whether CMC could actually improve on well-tried course production methods, and some might have been reluctant to invest time in a medium (computer conferencing) which would be liable to lead to protracted discussion of drafts of course material, and hence more work for individual authors in taking on board colleagues' comments.

The lack of interest in CoSy during the course production phase is reflected in the minutes of the regular production course team meetings, which contain only occasional references to the use of CMC on the course. However, the records of the meetings of the course maintenance team, set up once the course went live, contain an increasing number of references to CoSy, and during the second year of presentation of the course (1989), CMC-related issues became the main items of concern and attention. A number of reasons can be given for the growing significance attached to CMC by the presentation course team, despite the relatively small amount of time which students are expected to spend online (10-20 hours out of a total of about 400 hours):

• during the first year of the course, CoSy quickly became an invaluable and extremely rapid channel for students and tutors to notify problems to the course team; special conference topics were set up on CoSy for reporting problems with software, equipment, the network, and with the print materials (errata, delayed mailings, etc.), and other tutors and students, as well as members of the maintenance course team and the University's Academic Computing Service, could often provide answers through the same channel;

• some members of the course team who had contributed to the print and broadcast materials used a national forum conference on CoSy for running discussions on their parts of the course, as well as for up-dating the material; although only a minority of students contributed messages, a large proportion accessed and read the ensuing discussions;

• students were required to complete a written project on computer-mediated communication as part of their coursework, and two of the other assignments involved work related to CMC, so course team discussions concerning assignments invariably covered the use of CoSy;

• as the maintenance course team, and especially the course manager, became more at ease with CMC, the value of CoSy as a general course maintenance tool became increasingly apparent, not only for getting rapid feedback from students, but also for involving correspondence tutors and staff tutors, scattered all over the country, in decisions about revisions to the course, about preparation and grading of assignment and examination questions, and, in general, central-regional coordination;

• apart from the course assignments, CoSy is the only component of the course that can be changed from year to year, and is the only one which can be modified within a given presentation year, so there is a constant preoccupation with ways of using this flexibility to improve the course.

In conclusion, another factor which has influenced the increasing use of CoSy by the maintenance course team is the fact that it is largely composed of people who were not only committed to the teaching of the course, but were also favorably disposed to CMC from the start.

The Tutors

Tutors in the Open University system are, in a sense, mediators of the material prepared by the central course team—their role is to help students learn from the materials, through face-to-face tutorials, telephone contact, and written comments on students' monthly coursework assignments. They are also required to assess and grade their students' work, so a formal judgmental role has to be combined with that of learning facilitator.

Tutors are recruited and supported locally by full-time staff tutors, who are faculty members based in the University's 13 Regional Offices. Each tutor is responsible for 20-25 students in his or her locality, and will meet these students at occasional evening tutorials or day schools, as well as grade their coursework. Each tutor in a 400-hour full credit course in the Open University program is generally allocated about 14 hours for giving face-to-face tutorials, and will have maybe seven assignments to mark throughout the year (theoretically each one involving 20-25 scripts to mark) so the work is part-time. Many tutors, however, especially during the first year of a course, will spend far more time on helping their students than the approximate times for which the University pays them.

At the beginning of the first year of presentation of a course, new tutors generally attend a briefing meeting given by the course team and staff tutors. A de-briefing might also be organized at the end of the first year. During the year, especially in high-population courses which might have six or more tutors in a given region, day schools and briefing meetings might be arranged by staff tutors at regional offices. And samples of every tutor's marked scripts are selected automatically each month, photocopied, and sent to members of the maintenance course team for monitoring — a procedure designed both to identify severe and lenient tutors, as well as to provide guidance to new tutors on development of their correspondence marking skills. Comments from monitors are sent on to regional staff tutors, whose responsibility it is to take any necessary remedial action.

Apart from the features mentioned above, tutors in Open University courses normally have very little contact with each other, or with the course team, and very rarely meet students outside their own allocated group (unless the course is one of the few with a one-week residential school). Furthermore, as face-to-face tutorials are optional, and some students do not or cannot attend them, a tutor might never meet some of his or her allocated students. About one-third of the 120 undergraduate courses have fewer than 300 students each year, in which case there may only be one tutor per region—in such courses, because of the wider geographical spread of the students, tutorials cannot be organized very frequently, and there are few chances for a tutor to meet other tutors during the course of the teaching year.

Given the circumstances briefly sketched above, it might be reasonable to assume that CMC could play an important role in reducing tutors' isolation, in increasing their involvement with students and the course team, and in enriching their tutorial role—in short, in empowering them. So what in fact is happening?

DT200, with annual enrollments of up to 1500 students, requires around 70 tutors each year. The course is allocated 14 hours of group tuition time per tutor, generally divided 50/50 between face-to-face tuition and group tuition via CoSy. Tutors are also expected to deal with email messages from their students. In addition to being paid a tuition fee for 14 hours tutorial time, tutors are reimbursed for up to 20 hours online telephone costs.

Each tutor is moderator of a closed conference on CoSy, which is for the students in his or her tutor group. These tutor group conferences now generally have three or four topics, for chat, for discussion of the coursework assignments and tutorial meetings, and for the course project. During the first year of presentation, they also contain a separate topic for each block of the course (3), but these discussion topics rarely attracted many contributions, presumably because there were never enough active members in each group of 20-25 students. In addition to the local tutor group conferences, each tutor is also a member of one of six regional conferences, each one containing 6-8 tutors and up to 200 students. It is in these regional conferences that the main academic discussion of course themes is carried out on CoSy, within block related topics. Tutors are expected to contribute to regional conferences on a team teaching basis, organized cooperatively within each regional group.

During the first year of the course, the use of CoSy by tutors was extremely variable—about 30% of the tutors spent fewer than 10 hours online during the year, and another 30% spent over the 20 hours for which their connect costs were re-imbursed. A few tutors logged on nearly every day, while at the other extreme, a handful of tutors did not even fulfill a minimal contractual obligation to log on at least once before the due date for each of the coursework assignments. The picture was similar in the following year (1989), except that the proportion of tutors spending over 20 hours online was reduced to around 22% (this was probably due to a more efficient use of the system, especially in terms of increased offline reading and preparation of messages). The variability in take-up and use of CoSy by tutors can be attributed to a number of factors:

>•differences in attitude to CMC as a medium of communication—it is clear that some tutors adopted the medium enthusiastically, others had a fairly neutral or cautious attitude, and some disliked it (a similar range of attitudes is to be found among students);
>• differences in access conditions, in that some tutors had virtually unlimited free access from their own university offices via JANET (the Joint Academic NETwork that links

all British universities' computer systems), while, at the other extreme, some tutors were logging on from home at long-distance telephone call rates;
• differing levels of prior experience among tutors in using computers and computer software.

Tutors used CoSy in different ways. Some felt more at ease using email (e.g., for sending students comments on their coursework) than conferencing, especially in the first year (Thorpe, 1989). Clearly, one-to-one email is easier to assimilate to familiar communication modes (e.g., letter-writing) than computer conferencing is to, say, a traditional seminar or tutorial. Many tutors said they could see that conferencing had a great potential for group teaching, but only a few felt that they had used the medium satisfactorily in this way within the local or regional conferences, and they tended to be the tutors who were sufficiently enthusiastic about CMC to devote considerable amounts of time to the reading and preparation of messages.

Has CMC "empowered" the tutors? Some tutors (those who use the network a lot) believe so, for it has given them a chance to get far more involved in the course as a whole than would have been possible without access to CoSy. This increased involvement has taken a number of forms, from giving feedback to the course team in the closed tutors' conference, to contributing their own specialist knowledge to a wider audience than their own student group, and helping redesign the course's electronic environment for 1989. One tutor in 1988 set up a conference topic called *errata* for students and other tutors to post messages about mistakes in the printed course materials, which proved to be a valuable resource for the 1989 version of the course. Other tutors, together with their staff tutors, set up regional conferences to exchange ideas about teaching the course, to swap tips on effective conference moderation, and to organize events such as regional day schools. Tutors who were going to be absent for significant periods during the year were able to arrange for their students to be transferred electronically to another tutor, sometimes in an entirely different region of the country. And some were able to carry on their tutorial work despite being in isolated locations (one tutor who needed to make visits to oil rigs in the North Sea as part of his job was able to log on to CoSy from the rigs and deal with students' queries). And, of course, CMC enables tutors to stay in contact with their students regardless of where they are (one tutor had a student in Hong Kong in his group during 1989, and in 1990 the course was available to students resident in Belgium and Luxembourg).

There is no doubt that if CMC is adopted on a larger scale within the Open University system, and if it is given a specific tutorial role (in DT200, CoSy was as much an object of study—an example of Information Technology in action—as anything else), then it will inevitably lead to a change in the roles of tutors, and in the nature of their relationship to course team members and staff tutors. Thomas (1989) has pointed out that use of CMC could lead to the introduction of new types of courses at the University, where more resources would be put into online tutoring, and fewer into the preparation and production of expensive course materials. Such a model would be very appropriate for higher level low population courses, where tutors could rely on students having some level of specialist knowledge to contribute to online seminars and other collaborative activities. He also mentions the idea of an "electronic region" being established, which would pool the necessary human and logistical resources for courses, students, and tutors. Such a virtual region would, of course, cut across the existing regional organizational structure of the University, but might provide a more appropriate framework for tutors using CMC.

The Students

Studying at the Open University is very different from taking courses at a conventional, place-based institution. The student body is far more heterogeneous, with ages ranging from 19 to 90, and many students are in full-time employment and have domestic and family responsibilities. There are few opportunities for personal contact, discussion, and debate with other students, and normally a student would never meet any of the faculty or staff from the course team (unless the latter also happened to be teaching at a residential summer school or day school, or had also taken on a formal tutor role).

The reality of being an Open University student is well described by Ismail (1988), who stresses the need to organize time for study within a busy weekly schedule, to concentrate on the printed course materials, to make sure that monthly course assignments are completed on time, and to prepare for the end-of-course examination. Face-to-face tutorials and TV and radio broadcasts are often seen as optional luxuries, to be indulged in if time permits. From such a perspective, it might seem that many students would only make limited use of the CMC component in DT200, especially as the initial stages of learning to use the technology can be extremely time-consuming.

Students are introduced to CMC in the second month of the course, and part of the assignment for Block 2 requires them to submit evidence of use of CoSy to their tutor. Furthermore, the course project, work for which is done throughout much of the course, involves planning and writing a report on a chosen aspect of CMC. These factors have generally encouraged most students (with the exception of the 10% or so each year who drop out) to start to use CoSy, if only at a minimal level, within the first four months of the course. From this point on, the level of use, as for the tutors, is very variable—some students did little more than answer the welcoming email messages from their tutor and the course manager, and, at the other extreme, a small minority became very heavy users. In general, in the first year of the course, about one-third of the students spent fewer than 3 hours online, one-third between 3-10 hours, and one-third over 10 hours. Students had been advised in the course materials that about 10 hours online time would be sufficient for the required course work on CoSy.

This variability in use of CoSy by students cannot be explained purely by factors such as differences in the amount of time available, differences in access costs (nearly half of the students had to make long-distance calls to a dial-up node), and varying degrees of technical problems. Mason (1989b) points out that the limitations of CMC as a medium, at least as implemented in this course, were a major cause of disappointment among medium-to-low users of CoSy during the first year of the course. Many students started off with high expectations of CMC, and felt frustrated and disappointed when they logged on to the system to find very few or no new messages in their local tutor group conference, but large numbers of unread messages in the national conferences. Many of the messages in the large conferences were judged as peripheral, irrelevant, or junk, by many students, who resented spending time and money in accessing and downloading them, and then sorting through the downloaded material to find messages relevant to their own current preoccupations with the course. And some students did not like the recommended procedure of downloading new messages, reading and preparing comments off-line, and then logging on again to upload their messages, as they felt this reduced the spontaneity and excitement of the medium (even though it saved money on their telephone bill).

This situation improved in 1989, when the six regional conferences were set up, and students and tutors were recommended to use these as the main places for academic discussion of the principal themes and concepts of the course. These provided a larger critical mass of students and tutors for discussion than the local tutor group conferences, without going to the extreme of the national conferences, which all students and tutors could join. Analysis of these conferences showed that, on average:

- 15% of students never entered their regional conference (and many of these withdrew from the course, anyway);
- 50% "lurked" (visited the conference regularly to read new messages, but did not contribute any themselves);

• 35% contributed at least one message;
• 5% contributed 5 or more messages.

A content analysis of messages in two of the conferences showed that the single largest category of messages (40% of total messages) concerned course content and concepts; messages concerning technical and administrative issues formed the next largest category; about 15% of all messages were "chat" messages, and messages about CMC as a process totalled also around 15%. This shows an encouragingly low proportion of "chit-chat" messages (mostly restricted to the chat topic in each regional conference anyway), and a relatively high proportion of messages related to course themes and issues. However, a large proportion of the course-related messages was at the level of information exchange about, and broadening of, the material covered in the course units, typified by sequences of two or three messages in response to a query or problem raised by a student. Occasionally, protracted sequences of messages building on each other, going deeper into specific concepts, and developing into true discussion threads, did emerge, but this was not the typical picture. To put this into perspective, however, one might be inclined to ask how many face-to-face tutorials develop into prolonged interactive and constructive exchanges, bringing significant new depth into the discussion?

CoSy is presented in the DT200 course not only as an object of study, but also as a vehicle for tutorial discussion, and as a means of obtaining help from one's tutors and from other students. So students are likely to compare CMC with other, more traditional, channels of communication in making any judgments about the medium, even though it is qualitatively quite different from face-to-face, telephone, or written communication. As part of the course project, students are asked to complete and upload a questionnaire concerning their views on CMC, and there are several questions which ask them to compare CMC with other interactive channels used in distance education. It is interesting to note that, of the 790 students who uploaded their questionnaire data in the middle of the course in 1989, 35% found CMC as good or better a means of getting help or moral support as telephoning their tutor, and 43% could say that CMC was as good or better a medium for intellectual exchange than a face-to-face tutorial. A much smaller percentage (13%), however, rated CMC as being better or as good as face-to-face tutorials as a means of socializing. Such comparisons, although they beg the question of the significance of comparing three qualitatively and structurally dissimilar media of communication, are encouraging in that they show the development of relatively positive attitudes towards CMC after only a very limited exposure to the medium (the questions were answered only 3 months or so after students started to use CoSy).

Has the use of computer conferencing "empowered" Open University students? One of the questions in the project questionnaire touches on this issue (see Table 1).

Table 1: Attitudes Towards CMC (DT200 project questionnaire, 1989, n=789)

Does your own experience generally support or contradict the following suggestions about computer-mediated communication?

	Agree	Disagree	Uncertain
(i) Individuals can participate more equally in electronic than in face-to-face communication.	56%	26%	18%
(ii) Computer communication is depersonalizing.	59%	24%	17%
(iii) Computer conferencing encourages individual assertiveness.	35%	32%	33%
(iv) Personal interaction is more difficult with computer communication because of the lack of contextual and verbal feedback.	79%	10%	11%

Students were asked whether they agreed or disagreed with four statements about personal and inter-personal aspects of CMC as a communication medium. Well over half the respondents (56%) felt that people can "participate more equally in electronic than in face-to-face communication," and 35% found it "encourages individual assertiveness." Both of these might be taken as indices of the medium's "empowering" potential. But a high proportion of students (59%) found CMC "depersonalizing," and considered that "personal interaction becomes more difficult" (79%).

However, as with the tutors, a significant minority of students has developed very positive attitudes towards CMC along a number of dimensions (again, see Table 1), and these students have become heavy users of CoSy. In 1989, for example, 13% of the 787 students who uploaded their project questionnaire data said that they used CoSy often for contacting other students, and 12% said they would be "very enthusiastic" about continuing to use CoSy after the end of the course, provided they had the necessary equipment (while 46% said they would be "quite interested.") Many of the enthusiasts have obtained their own modems and joined the increasing number of DT200 "alumni." Among the keenest users of CoSy in 1988 was a student who set up an electronic newsletter, with contributions from staff, tutors, and other students. This particular student claims that "the system is a marvelous socializing medium, and many of these (online) friendships are followed up offline...it provides a real feeling of involvement and...creates a unique electronic campus with much of the variety of the real thing" (Malone, 1989). Another regular user, a disabled housebound student unable to attend face-to-face tutorials, has said that..."the sort of contact available via CoSy has made me feel part of a real university for the first time" (4); this student set up and ran a "chatline" for other students which became one of the liveliest and most interesting sites of social discourse on the system during 1988. Other students set up electronic self-help groups on CoSy, using the private conversation facility, for exchanging views on the course materials, and providing each other with advice on the practical work and assignments. Yet others gave valuable advice on problems with software and practical work in the national course conferences on CoSy (the practical and gremlins topics in the national forum conference in 1988 together attracted 950 messages, the majority from students).

In general, it seems clear that a significant minority of students taking DT200 felt that CMC had given them an enhanced opportunity to contribute and share their own ideas and experiences in a dynamic way. Many of the students had specialist knowledge of particular areas covered in the course, because of their work background (e.g., as British Telecom engineers, computer programmers and systems analysts, office managers, and other IT professionals), and their contributions were often highly valued and relevant. Students who had previously studied the Social Sciences Foundation Course were able to help technology-oriented students with problems about social science concepts and jargon, and vice versa. Without CoSy, much of this sharing and exchange would have been impossible. At the level of interpersonal contact and mutual support, a significant minority of students used CoSy and the potential of computer networking to make serendipitous encounters with other students and tutors outside their own restricted tutorial group, and thus vastly broaden their range of social contacts.

Conclusions

At the beginning of this chapter it was suggested that CMC might help remedy two of the major drawbacks of multi-media distance education courses for mass audiences—namely the "inert" nature of the pre-packaged course materials, often designed for repeated presentations over several years, and the paucity of opportunities for interactive discussion and collaboration among and between students and tutors.

The experience of using CMC over a two-year period in adjunct mode in the DT200 course at the Open University has certainly demonstrated that it is possible to introduce up-dating material and items of topical interest into a course through CMC, and, moreover, that this can be done by students and tutors just as well as by the central course team. Topics in both the national forum conference, and in the regional conferences, often included references to, and citations from, newspaper, magazine, and journal articles, as well as TV programs, relevant to themes then being discussed in the course. And course team members responsible for the writing of particular blocks and units often used the national conferences to update their material. Likewise, CMC provided the opportunity for students and tutors to interact with each other on a scale which would be quite impossible in a conventional Open University course.

However, it is also clear that a large proportion of students and tutors in the course did not play an active part in taking advantage of these opportunities—other than by reading messages posted by others in the local, regional, and national conferences. Furthermore, course team members are reluctant to make a major use of CMC for updating and complementing the printed and broadcast course materials, as this will be perceived as increasing the students' workload (yet more material to read) as well as increasing the cost of the course to students (through increased connect time charges). Any updated or revised material considered to be essential is printed and sent through the mail, so that all students will receive it, not just those who use CoSy regularly.

In terms of the use of CMC as an object of study, an example of it in action, the application on DT200 was certainly a success. Contrary to early expectations, students and tutors experienced few major technical difficulties in using a modem and comms software to connect to the University network (once they had gotten over the initial hurdles). It has proved possible for large numbers to learn how to use email and conferencing successfully, at a distance, by following the instructions and exercises included in the print and audiocassette course materials, and by using the menu-driven front-end provided as part of the course software. For example, 95% of students said they felt comfortable about sending email messages, and 86% were comfortable about contributing messages to a conference, after using the system 10 times or less. It should be noted that, in the great majority of cases, this rapid mastery of the basic repertoire of skills needed to use CoSy was achieved with little or no face-to-face training (5).

However, it is clear that the full potential of CMC as a medium for educational communication and collaboration in the distance learning environment has not been realized in DT200, and indeed, could not be, given the marginal and ambiguous role which is assigned to it in the course. A case, and a strong one, can be made for using CMC in adjunct mode in traditional multi-media OU courses for particular groups of students (the housebound, those unable to attend tutorials, overseas students, certain categories of disabled students), and for those who are enthusiastic about the medium, and want to use it as an optional facility for networking and for running online self-help groups. However, the realization of the full educational potential of CMC in the Open University context would require the development of a new type of course design, with less emphasis being placed on pre-packaged materials, and more emphasis on the role of the tutor and on the contributions which students can make from their own knowledge and experience. Such a model would be very appropriate for many of the low population third- and fourth-level specialist courses in the undergraduate program, as well as for post-experience and post-graduate courses.

Any widespread application within the Open University program of a course design built around the model of an "electronic seminar," with opportunities for extended discussion and collaborative work would, however, require certain technological and economic developments. At the very minimum, the University would need to provide local call access to its network from anywhere in the country: at the moment, the cost of such a facility in the UK is prohibitive. Secondly, the University would need to pay tutors more for the increased time they would be spending on their work, both online and off-line: CMC is a labor-intensive medium, and realization of its full potential would mean a shift of financial resources from course production to course presentation. Thirdly, it would be highly desirable for students and tutors to have a home workstation which would combine CMC transparently with a number of other computer-based tools (graphics, an ideas processor, a word-processor, course-based teaching software, etc.) and which would also contain software for local selection, organization, and retrieval of relevant material downloaded from the conferencing system. This, although it has major cost implications, would go a long way towards dealing with the complaints made by many students and tutors on DT200 about the difficulty of locating personally useful and relevant information in the course conferences. An operational design for such a workstation tailored to the needs of distance learners (a "Thought Box") has been developed at the Open University (Alexander and Lincoln, 1989).

In the final analysis, the issue of the future development of CMC in a mass distance education institution such as the Open University comes down to one of cost. The cost structure of the Open University, which enables it to produce graduates at about one-half of the cost per graduate of a traditional place-based institution (Perry, 1976, p. 239), is based on the amortization of high course development costs over large numbers of students, with repeated presentations of courses which, as far as is possible, have a standard structure and format (Rumble, 1988). The introduction of different course models, especially if they offer choices to students and tutors in the media used, will inevitably push unit costs upwards.

Experience with the use of CMC at the Open University so far suggests, not surprisingly, that there are wide variations in preferences for this medium. Some students and tutors want to use conferencing actively, and feel that it has "empowered" them, and brought a qualitatively new dimension into their experience of distance learning and teaching. At the other end of the spectrum are those students who are neutral or disinterested in CMC, and are quite happy to study essentially on their own, with little recourse to other students and their tutors: their approach tends to be highly instrumental, and heavily grade-oriented. The major challenge for the future development of mass distance education institutions will be to find ways of benefiting from the new communications technologies which will not only provide a diversity of course models to satisfy differing students' requirements, but will also maintain costs at a viable level.

Notes

(1) To give an idea of the scale of the course production operation, the DT200 materials include:
• 28 printed self-study units, each ranging in length from 32 to 92 pages, and written entirely by the course team.
• a course reader of over 300 pages, containing articles selected by the course team.
• 16 TV programs, 8 radio programs, and several hours of audio-cassette material, again all originated by the course team.
• many printed supplementary materials (course guide, broadcast notes, project notes, assignments, tutor notes, examination questions, and marking guides, etc.).
• 4 commercial software packages, on floppy disks, plus their reference manuals.
• a menu-driven front end to CoSy, on disk, developed by the course team.
• software on the VAX cluster, including modifications to CoSy, a course "shell," and a central data-base, so students could upload and download data needed for their course project.
• a modem, selected after public bidding process, and specially modified for use in the course (students are expected to obtain their own PC's and printers, either by purchase, or through a rental scheme operated under contract to the University).

(2) See Kaye, A., Mason, R., and Harasim, L. (1989) for a discussion and analysis of the use of computer conferencing for academic collaboration and administration.

(3) DT200 is composed of seven "blocks" of course material, each

representing about one month's work for the students. Each block includes a social science strand, a technology strand, an application strand, and a practical work strand. Five main application areas are covered in Blocks 2-6: IT (Information Technology) in the home; in banking, finance, and retailing; in education and training; in manufacturing; and in government. Blocks 1 and 7 are, respectively, an introduction to the course ("Technology, people, and issues") and a conclusion.

The course materials for each block include self-study texts, articles from the course reader (Information Technology: Social Issues), television programs, audio cassettes, computer software, and course assignments.

(4) See message No. 5 in the Prologue to Mason and Kaye (Eds.), (1989).

(5) Some tutors and staff tutors do organize a short "hands on" induction session at the beginning of the course for those in difficulty, but the great majority of students learn how to use CoSy on their own, at home.

References

Alexander, G., and Lincoln, C. (1989). The thought box: A computer-based communication system for distance learning. In R. Mason and A. Kaye (Eds.), *Mindweave: Communication, computers, and distance education*, 86-100. Oxford: Pergamon.

Feenberg, A. (1989). A guide to the pragmatics of computer-mediated communication. *Semiotica*, 75-3/4, 257-278.

Harasim, L. (1987). Teaching and learning online: Issues in computer-mediated graduate courses. *Canadian Journal of Educational Communication*, *16* (2), 117-135.

Harasim, L. (1989). On-line education: A new domain. In R. Mason and A. Kaye (Eds.), *op cit*, 50-62.

Henri, F. (1988). Distance education and computer-assisted communication. *Prospects, 18* (1), 85-90. Paris: UNESCO.

Hiltz, S. (1986). The "virtual classroom": Using computer mediated communication for university teaching. *Journal of Communication*, Spring 1986.

Ismail, N. (1988). A year in the life of an open university student in the United Kingdom. *Prospects, 18* (2), 255-265. Paris: UNESCO.

Kaye, A. (1987). Introducing computer-mediated communication into a distance education system. *Canadian Journal of Educational Communication, 16* (2), 153-166.

Kaye, A., Mason, R., and Harasim, L. (1989). Computer conferencing in the academic environment. *CITE Paper No. 91*. Milton Keynes, England: Open University.

Lamy, T. (1985). La télématique: Un outil convivial? In F. Henri and A. Kaye (Eds.), *Le savoir de domicile: Pédagogie et problématique de la formation a distance*, 303-328. Les Presses de l'Universite du Québec: Québec.

Malone, K. (1989). On the electronic campus. *Personal Commuting*, 54-56.

Mason, R. (1989a). An evaluation of CoSy on an Open Univer-
       sity course. In R. Mason and A. Kaye (Eds.), *Mindweave:*
       Communication, computers, and distance education, 115-
       145. Oxford: Pergamon.

Mason, R. (1989b). A case study of the use of computer conferencing
       at the Open University. Unpublished Doctoral Dissertation.
       Milton Keynes, England: Open University.

Mason, R., and Kaye, A. (Eds.). (1989). *Mindweave: Communi-*
       cation, computers, and distance education. Oxford:
       Pergamon.

Perry, W. (1976). *Open University : A personal account by the*
       first vice-chancellor. Milton Keynes, England: Open
       University Press.

Rumble, G. (1988). The economics of mass distance education.
       Prospects, *18* (1), 91-102. Paris: UNESCO.

Thomas, R. (1989). The implications of electronic communica-
       tion for the Open University. In R. Mason and A. Kaye,
       (Eds.), *op cit*, 166-177.

Thorpe, M. (1989). The tutor perspective on CMC in DT200.
       CITE Paper No. 76. Milton Keynes, England: Open
       University.

Winkelmans, T. (1988). Educational computer conferencing: An
       application of analysis methodologies to a structured
       small group activity. Unpublished Master's Thesis.
       University of Toronto.

5

Instructional Gaming Through Computer Conferencing

Frederick L. Goodman

General Background

The aim of this chapter is not only to describe the development and operation of what has come to be called the Interactive Communication Simulations (ICS) program that offers schools around the world an opportunity to participate in a series of "global classrooms," but it is also to project a series of activities that may soon be undertaken in conjunction with the ICS enterprise. The underlying rationale for the entire program will be sketched; the reaction of teachers who have participated in the exercises will be reported; and the concerns as well as the hopes for the future of those most responsible for its operations will be delineated.

ICS, in its simplest sense, is the combination of two lines of work that were, for a number of years, running parallel to one another. One involved the development of an increasingly sophisticated kind of role-playing game dealing with the subject of the Arab-Israeli conflict. This was started in 1974 by Edgar C. Taylor, Jr., then a Graduate Student Teaching Assistant for a course taught in the political science department of The University of Michigan on the Arab-Israeli conflict. For a number of years Leonard Suransky, a graduate student in the School of Education, was deeply involved in the design and conduct of the simulation that was offered each year in that course, and wrote a dissertation about his experience, appearing in 1980. An Arab-Israeli simulation has been

101

conducted in conjunction with the course on that subject taught by one political science professor or another every year since 1974.

The other line of work, starting in 1975, involved the development of the computer-conferencing system that is known as Confer. Robert Parnes, also a graduate student in the School of Education at Michigan at the time, began the design of Confer at the suggestion of Professor Merrill M. Flood, who was conducting a seminar on university governance. Within a few years Confer became a commercially available system used extensively by the U.S. Army and major corporations, but it was also supported at The University of Michigan by Dr. Parnes, where it has undergone continuous development. By the fall of 1983, it became clear that Confer could be used as a medium for the exchange of messages in an exercise such as the Arab-Israeli conflict simulation.

Up until the end of 1983 the Arab-Israeli conflict "game," as it was frequently called, had always been played over a long weekend; that is, from Friday evening through Sunday afternoon. This would take place about nine or ten weeks into a fourteen-week course, allowing the students plenty of preparation time in which they were to write what came to be called "Country Profiles" and "Role Profiles," describing not only the general attributes of the country that they were to represent, but also the characteristics of the individual leaders in that country whom the students were to portray during the exercise. From the outset a very important dimension of the simulation was that students were to play the role of specific, "real" characters, attempting to act as much as possible the way they thought that person would act in a specific situation, even if, in the real world, that person had never been in a situation quite like the one facing him or her in the simulated world. The intention was not only to create as much verisimilitude as possible during the game, but also it was to create the expectation that students indulge in a maximum amount of study in preparation for the game. They were not to behave like some generic President of the United States would behave, or the way they thought they themselves might behave; they were to behave the way Nixon or Carter or Reagan or Bush would behave under particular circumstances. With the exception of roles developed for "private emissaries" who work behind the scenes to accomplish goals that tend to be handled that way, all the characters played are actual, real-world people. The Role Profiles of the "private emissaries" are essentially pieces of fiction. All the other Role Profiles are written and evaluated in the same way a brief paper in a political science class would be handled; that is, a premium is placed on thorough research and precise writing.

On two occasions, computers had been moved into the classrooms that were used for the weekend games, and Confer had been used successfully as an experiment to see if an exercise could be run more smoothly with the aid of electronic messaging as contrasted to the conventional procedure of having a fleet of "runners" carrying hand written or typed messages up and down the corridors connecting the rooms. Thus in some ways it was a relatively small step to recognize that the simulation might just as well be played with participants who were at great distances from one another rather than in adjacent classrooms, and, in almost as obvious a fashion, that the exercise could be extended over a longer time period, capitalizing on the central idea of computer-conferencing, namely, its "store and forward" capacity.

The occasion for recognizing this potential arose when the Professional Development Office of the School of Education highlighted the fact that there was an expressed need throughout the State of Michigan for improved programs for students designated as "gifted and talented," for more creative uses of computers in classrooms, and, quite simply, for programs that would serve to better motivate students of all kinds to spend more time on their studies. It seemed possible that a secondary school version of the Arab-Israeli exercise might meet all these objectives and do so in a cost-effective manner. The Coordinator of the "Gifted and Talented" Program for the State of Michigan's Department of Education assisted with the location of a small set of schools, and the first run of the game occurred in the Spring of 1984, several of the participating teachers and some Gifted and Talented Consultants having visited Ann Arbor in November of 1983 to observe the university students' weekend simulation.

In a very real sense, the program simply continued to grow almost continuously from then on, adding not only more and, in some instances, very different kinds of schools each term, but also gradually adding exercises covering very different subject matter and, in some cases, utilizing pedagogical strategies quite different from the role-playing, or as they came to be called, "character-playing" games. Hundreds of schools from fourteen foreign countries and a total of twenty-two states have participated in seven very different exercises. Private schools have played along with public schools. Urban, suburban, small town, and rural schools have been involved. Many overseas schools are associated with the U.S. Department of Defense; others are American Independent Schools. So far the only countries to have regular, indigenous schools participate are Canada, Germany, Israel, and Singapore. Students have included those identified as "gifted and talented" and as "emotionally disturbed," along with hearing-impaired students. Students enrolled in adult education classes have participated right along with those of traditional age. In addition there have been a number of college students participating in games that are primarily for pre-collegiate students. In some cases this involves students in social studies methods classes at the University of Michigan who are playing in order to familiarize themselves with this teaching technique and to get a first-hand look at what middle and high school students can do when participating in an exercise of this type. In other cases they are simply classes of college students taught by instructors who became familiar with the program in one way or another and wanted to include the simulation in their teaching efforts. The exact number of students involved can only be estimated since in most instances the number of people playing each role is not known back at ICS "headquarters." As of the summer of

1990 the total number of students participating in the networked games was estimated in the thousands.

But another major feature of ICS needs to be identified before providing more detail on the nature of this growth and development. After two years of experience with pre-collegiate games played over great distances and over a much greater time period, typically three to five weeks as contrasted to a single weekend for the collegiate games, an experiment was launched in 1987 utilizing Confer as a medium to play games on campus over similarly long periods of time. It took very little time at all to realize that there was an enormous difference not only in the quantity of messages that were exchanged but also in the quality of the messages that students composed for one another. Participants can give careful reflection to the positions they wish to take, do additional research, and spend more time on composing their messages when the game stretches out over a number of weeks. On many occasions face-to-face meetings have been arranged at the request of players, so that dimension has not been completely lost despite the predominant use of computer-mediated communications.

One of the most important features of the ICS initiative is the richness of the link between The University of Michigan and the high schools and middle schools that participate at the pre-collegiate level. As will be described, this has gone well beyond the initial link, which was the use of country and role profiles prepared by Michigan students as the essence of the notebooks provided for the use of younger students, who would not have the access to library resources that the college students had when it was time to prepare to participate in the simulation.

The Arab-Israeli Conflict Simulation

Since a great deal of the development of the overall ICS program is associated with the Arab-Israeli simulation, which for several terms was the only exercise available to students, it is reasonable to provide a fuller explanation of that game as the first step in sketching the nature of the approach. Indeed the original meaning of the letters "ICS" was "International Conflict Simulation," and that is all that we thought that we were doing. It was only when a simulation dealing with the United States Constitutional Convention was conceived and developed that the name was changed to its present form, namely, "Interactive Communication Simulations." As is so often the case with acronyms, we found that our activities were identified simply by the letters "ICS," and there was a sense in which we could not stop people from referring to whatever we were doing by using that label. Thus we needed to find a more accurate set of words to fit the acronym. Indeed there may soon have to be another change of a similar nature since our activities already extend beyond the domain of "simulations" and are likely to do so even more in the near future, as will be described.

Perhaps the simplest way to describe the Arab-Israeli "game" (for, as indicated previously, whether we choose to refer to the activity as a "game" or not, it tends to be called that by others) is to say that for a relatively small sum of money we will "sell a school a country in the Middle East" and the students in that school can try to run it for a term. This description is not entirely accurate, but the image it conjures up is not too erroneous. It is not accurate because not all the schools are assigned countries in the Middle East. The United States and the U.S.S.R. are always in the game. Further, one school gets the "West Bank" and another the "PLO," neither of which is a "country." For several terms there were two "Lebanon" teams in the game, one representing the Moslem factions in Lebanon, the other the Christians. That the actual number of teams in the game can change a little from year to year illustrates the dynamic nature of the exercise. Its structure stays more or less the same but changes are made in response to the political realities in that part of the world.

From the outset the charge to the individual school covered not only the costs associated with the notebook that students needed to help them know how to participate realistically, and the supervision provided by people at the university, but it also covered computer costs and telecommunications costs exclusive of those incurred to reach the nearest node on one of the many networks that could be used to reach The University of Michigan mainframe computer. The initial charge in 1984 was $150 per team, a team consisting of five roles representing major political figures in each country, roles that could either be played by five individual students or by a whole class of students (a group of five or six students, for example, getting together to play the role of a single character such as Yasir Arafat). Sometimes a school would decide to have two teams in a single class, perhaps both of them being the same country in different games, or two different countries, each of which would participate in a different game. These decisions were worked out between the teacher in the school most responsible for the exercise, a person called the "Team Facilitator," and the director of the simulation, Dr. Taylor. In the early days a few schools even had more than two teams per class, but this practice soon was seen to be impractical on many grounds. Indeed in the early days some teams had more or fewer than five roles, but this was standardized early on for a variety of reasons. The cost of a team at this point is $250 per term, with the distinct possibility of a price increase on the horizon.

Given that there are, typically, eleven teams in a single Arab-Israeli game, one of the difficult problems associated with launching a team's activities has always been getting just the right number of multiples of eleven teams. A big step in solving this problem was to ask schools to mark on their registration forms whether or not they would consider taking additional teams **free** if that would round out an additional game. Nevertheless, the beginning of each term usually marks a scramble to solicit new schools and/or the need to tell teachers that they cannot have exactly the number of teams that they prefer. As we soon were to realize, the larger the number of teams per game, the worse this problem became.

There are three kinds of messages that a team must get ready to exchange. One is a "diplomatic message" exchanged directly between one character and another, e.g., a message sent by Bush to Gorbachev. Another is a "press release" sent by a team, i.e., in most instances by a country; a message which ends up as part of what has come to be called the "ICS Wire Service." The final kind of message is called an "Action Form," the nature of which first requires a description of someone known as a "controller."

Initially, Edgar Taylor "controlled" all the games since the first term back in 1984. Very soon it became clear that it would not be possible for one person to control the volume of activity that ICS was capable of generating. Hence the introduction of the use of veterans of the collegiate game as controllers of the pre-collegiate games. Between 1974 and 1984, veterans of the on-campus weekend games would volunteer to help run the "control room" where runners (typically elementary or junior high students who were known to Dr. Taylor) brought multiple copies of all the messages of all kinds. It had become clear that the game had such an appeal to its participants that many students liked to have something to do with it long after they had finished the course in which they had played it, and they would assist Dr. Taylor in the "control room." Thus when we began the secondary-school games, it was simply a matter of working out an arrangement for offering credit in the School of Education to students who would sign up for a course in which they would serve as controllers to the high school and middle school students. By so doing they would be pursuing their knowledge of Arab-Israeli conflict related matters in greater depth as well as learning how to translate these highly technical and emotionally loaded issues into terms that could be understood by younger students. All controllers engage in a weekly seminar conducted by Dr. Taylor to discuss how to help their charges prepare for the game; how to help motivate inactive individuals, teams, or even entire games; how to try to alter inappropriate behavior by youngsters who might be "out of role" or perhaps simply too naive or rude; and ultimately how to assist with a debriefing in which the group was to try to come to grips with what they had learned about all manner of things.

It soon developed that controllers were split into two groups, those who alone or with a classmate controlled an entire game, seeing all the messages exchanged by all members of all teams, and those who came to be called "National Security Advisors," who were privy only to those messages that were sent or received by all the different "Syrias," for example, in the several different games. At the high water mark of the Arab-Israeli exercise, before there were other ICS exercises, there were seven simultaneous games, four at the high school level, three at the middle school level. It would be the controller(s) of the game as a whole who would receive the "Action Form" referred to above.

In essence, an Action Form was to be sent by a team whenever it wanted to do anything other than "talk." If a team or some of its members wanted to take action, such as move troops or attempt a coup, they could not simply announce that they "had done so." Instead the student or students had to fill in a form on which were described the alternatives that had been considered, why a particular option had been selected, what the odds of success associated with this option were, what the costs and benefits were should the move go well ... or fail, and so on. The controller for that game would then consider all this, ask the students for additional information, consult with his or her fellow controllers, etc., and finally announce via the "ICS Wire Service" what the outcome of such a request for action "actually was." Fairly early in the history of using undergraduate students to control such games, we were persuaded by the controllers themselves to let the students have their way as much as possible. That is, the goal became to reason with them for a while, but if they persisted in doing something that the controllers felt was "off the wall" or unrealistic, let the action at least be attempted, and then show them through the report in the Wire Service that the consequences of such a move were far different than they might have suspected. Thus the controllers stayed in charge of the game at the level of keeping it "on the rails" of realism, but the students were hardly ever told that "they couldn't do something" that they really wanted to try doing. In the six years of experience with the simulations, there have never been serious difficulties in exercising judgment along these lines satisfactorily.

Game controllers, then, in addition to handling Action Forms, were to review all diplomatic messages, **after** they were sent, and post all press releases in the Wire Service, reviewing them for coherence and plausibility **before** so doing. This allowed the game to proceed at a brisk pace without running the risk of a deluge of diplomatic messages being "bottle-necked" by a controller, yet keeping inappropriate press releases from ever getting out where everybody would see them and all sorts of problems would be involved in bringing things back in line. In other words, an inappropriate diplomatic message would only go to one character, so if that had to be "retracted" or explained, the focus for so doing was very clear and concise. Likewise, the "guilty party" would also be only one "character," be that one student or several playing the role of that character, not a whole team or classroom, so an explanation to that party could be handled directly with a single message. Of course the Team Facilitator in that school might also be alerted to problems of this type if need be.

Further, it soon became desirable to ask the game controllers to compose and send to all Team Facilitators in their game a "State of the Game" report at the end of the week. This could be used by the students' teacher in many, many ways, for it not only provided him or her with an overview of the "Middle East," but it also contained information about the relative activity or inactivity of that teacher's team. From the vantage point of those responsible for the whole ICS operation, the quality of such reports also provided extremely valuable information on the performance of the controllers themselves.

The notion of using controllers as "National Security Advisors" came about in two ways. Initially, students in a participating high school came up with the idea that they might like to play some role in subsequent terms other than just a "player." They might like to help out, to coach other players. Although this feature never really worked out, it became clear almost immediately that there was something to be said for helping some if not all teams play their roles accurately, imaginatively, and above all, vigorously. Indeed one of the most pressing problems was, and remains, the problem of an inactive team whose lack of participation can ruin a whole game. The "National Security Advisor" concept provides a way of handling that problem, although if it becomes so extreme that the "NSA" must actually take over for a defunct team it is a kind of "hollow victory." Nevertheless, the structure is there for the game to go on in the worst case. Much more likely, the role of the NSA is to help students understand what is going on in "their world," to help evaluate the behavior of other countries or individual leaders, to suggest options that might be open to members of the team, etc. In many ways this is exactly what an actual National Security Advisor does in the "real world."

Armed with the assistance of both Game Controllers and National Security Advisers, a Team Facilitator, that is a regular classroom teacher (or perhaps in some cases a counsellor or someone else in the school system), need not feel that he or she must know a great deal about the Arab-Israeli conflict in order to venture forth into these uncharted waters. Still, there can be an enormous amount for the Team Facilitator to do, not the least of which is to oversee the use of the microcomputers used to compose, send, and receive the messages that form the substance of the ICS process. Over the six years that ICS has been in existence, considerable strides have been made in familiarizing the public-at-large with the notion of sending and receiving word-processed messages via telephone lines. But access to telephones in public schools remains difficult in all but the most unusual circumstances, and the variety of procedures and protocols with which a teacher must become familiar once a phone line, a modem, and a microcomputer have been procured can be intimidating to all but the most patient and resourceful teachers. One of the things that most interests those of us concerned with using this complex teaching technique has to do with teachers' perceptions of whether or not the demands placed upon them are worth it or not. That topic will be assessed in the section below on Teachers' Responses.

A rather large number of small but important "technical" changes have been made during the evolution of the program. For example, a "communications-matrix" was designed and implemented to make it impossible for any one player to communicate with any but a small set of other players. This was done not only to keep the games more realistic by preventing people who would not ordinarily communicate directly with one another in the real world from doing so in the simulation, but it also provided a natural way for any one student to begin to learn all the new information that might be necessary to learn in order to play well. If you could only communicate directly with six other characters, then you could begin by reading those role-profiles in the notebook in addition to your own. Since all of the characters on your team interacted with different sets of six people, and you needed to interact with all your "teammates," the circle of what you would eventually come to know would grow quite naturally. And, the communications-matrix also served an important role in facilitating the sending and receiving of copies of messages to Game Controllers and National Security Advisers.

A number of adjustments were also made in the way individual users of the system would be able to find their way around within the system in order to send messages and to receive the messages that were targeted for them, while maintaining efficient contact with the central computer. The normal computer-conferencing system gives a discrete identification number to each user, and that person's public and private communications are tracked via that number. For reasons of efficiency from a technical point of view, a bookkeeping point of view, and from the viewpoint of a teacher who was trying to keep up with several classes' performance, a school ended up getting a single "sign-on" number. Not only did different characters within a game use that number, but the same number was also used by participants in different games, so Confer had to be adjusted to provide switching techniques and prompts to help people keep track of "who they were" and "where they were" in the system.

Further, it became clear that it would be extremely useful to automatically record certain aspects of the system so as to make it easier to keep track of which teams were doing what. An "Activity Log" was developed so that all aspects of the system could be monitored and compared more easily with an eye to getting information to Team Facilitators in time to influence their ability to help their teams perform better, as well as to those monitoring the efforts of the controllers and responsible for keeping track of costs.

An enormous portion of the development of the technical side of the program was made possible by the work of Clancy Wolf, a graduate student in the School of Education at The University of Michigan. His ability to relate to the needs and concerns of the Team Facilitators throughout the entire global network has been extraordinary. This has meant supporting a wide range of micro-computers, wordprocessing software, modems, and communications software. Further it required mastering the intricacies of establishing connections between schools and The University of Michigan's IBM 3090-600E mainframe computer via a variety of telecommunications carriers. Different countries' requirements had to be assessed and a range of alternatives had to be considered before recommendations to individual schools could be made. In addition, he developed and supervises the Environmental Decisions exercise. For the last several years he has been very ably assisted by a Michigan undergraduate, Markus Mueller, who not only developed software to facilitate the operation of the entire system, but also played a central role in facilitating the many on-campus games at the University level that provide the entire ICS system with much of its strength.

Some of the technical changes that were made came in response to problems posed by exercises other than the Arab-Israeli conflict simulation, but, with a few exceptions that will be noted in the next section, in many ways the fundamental infrastructure of ICS was determined by the needs of the Arab-Israeli game.

A final note before proceeding to descriptions of other ICS exercises. Almost from the outset, a policy of not revealing the identity of students participating in the role-playing games rapidly came into effect. That is, until the debriefing phase of the exercise began, no participant or Team Facilitator knew anything about the personal characteristics of another person or persons playing a particular leader or the characteristics of a set of other students representing the leadership of a country. In essence, the debriefing period would tend to begin with questions like, "Who are you **really**?" This offers fascinating possibilities for overcoming stereotypes based on race, gender, socio-economic class, and geography.

Other Exercises

The ICS exercise most like the Arab-Israeli conflict simulation deals with a United States Constitutional Convention. The basic idea was to identify a fairly large number of individuals who had played important roles in shaping the country's constitutional history, and then have them participate in a new constitutional convention. In part this was inspired by the attention given to constitutional issues during the bicentennial celebration of the constitution in the mid-1980's. In part it was a reaction to inquiries from schools that were interested in the idea of computer-conferenced role-playing games, but wanted something a bit closer to their curricula than the topics covered in the Arab-Israeli game.

With funding provided by the Exxon Education Foundation, the design of the simulation began in the summer of 1986. The basic problem to be solved involved the notion that history itself is analogous to a "play of a game," as contrasted to "a game." A game is a series of *occasions for making* choices; a play of a game is a set of *particular* choices *made* on those occasions. History can be thought of as a set of choices that were made, or more appropriately, are alleged by historians to have been made, by people when they were presented with those choices. Once a particular option was exercised, the course of history flowed in that direction, not the direction that might have been taken if an alternative path had been chosen. If students make a dramatically different choice than did those present at the time at a particular "crossroads" in a game purporting to be historical, everything they did thereafter would have the potential of being very **non-historical**. The problem was to keep the exercises from deteriorating *either* into a morass of options that might be very far indeed from those which historians might think plausible, *or* into a "pseudo-game" in which the participants were not really allowed to make their own choices at critical junctures but rather were told what they must do if their play were to be kept realistic.

The solution developed for this involved the rather bizarre notion of transporting historical figures into the future, rather than simply transporting students into the past. To be sure, the student who was to role-play a particular historical character would have to *study* the past, but he or she would not have to *act* in the past nor would the many players participating in the exercise be responsible for keeping their version of the past sufficiently like the "real" past to satisfy those concerned with historical authenticity. This would be done by simply inviting all the people whose roles were to be played (almost all of whom were deceased) to attend a simulated constitutional convention in the "upcoming summer in Philadelphia." But how to select the individuals whose roles were to be played?

At the suggestion of a colleague in The University of Michigan's history department, Professor J. Mills Thornton, III, was approached to see if he would be willing to work with us to identify a set of people who could be said to represent many of the major issues influencing the course of the country's constitutional history. He agreed, and over the course of about two months, working in close association with Genevieve Berkhofer, an experienced social studies' educator extensively familiar with U. S. constitutional history, along with ICS staff members, he identified a list of 70 figures. These were organized into "delegations," each consisting of five people drawn from the entire 200-year period who could be said to have "something in common" relative to their positions on constitutional matters. Just what they had in common was left to the students, and one of the first things participants are asked to do is "name" their delegation in a way that might communicate why they might be treated as a "team." Further, each delegate was assigned to one of five different "drafting committees," e.g., working on the powers of the executive, the powers of the judiciary, federal-state relations, and so on. Actually, the first design featured ten drafting committees but this proved to be too fine-grained an exercise and after a term's experience, the simpler five-committee structure was adopted.

Essays identifying the major issues to be addressed by the drafting committees were prepared and then profiles of each of the delegates were developed. These emphasized aspects of the delegate's life and times that related to the issues he or she would be asked to consider as a member of a particular drafting committee. Constitutions from other countries and other times were examined to identify passages that could be excerpted and included in the notebook provided for participating schools, each entry aimed at suggesting points that the students might consider as they went about their work as members of a particular drafting committee. This work was done by graduate and undergraduate students under the leadership of Ms. Berkhofer.

To run an exercise, the fourteen delegations constituting a "game" are assigned to fourteen different schools and then charged with working together to make any changes in the constitution that they would recommend, keeping in mind that the participants are to "stay in role"; that is, be as true as they can be to the character of the person being "played" and the constraints that person would be under at that period in history. As with the Arab-Israeli simulation, a particular character such as Thomas Jefferson or Martin Luther King, Jr., might be played by one student or as many as five or six, depending on how a school chooses to utilize the exercise. Ultimately each delegation votes as a whole on the recommended changes, producing a "new constitution."

Controllers guide each game in a manner similar to that explained in the Arab-Israeli simulation, but instead of acting as "National Security Advisors," the college students working with the younger students are placed strategically on drafting committees, actually playing the roles of several delegates. The idea is to ensure that there is a way for each committee to get started and an inconspicuous way to raise issues that the ICS staff would like to see the participants consider if that kind of additional stimulus is needed. As with all delegates, the identity of these "controller" delegates is kept anonymous during the actual play of the game. In the debriefing, their role in the game is not emphasized and participants tend not even to know that some roles have been played in this fashion.

Once the viability of using historical figures in such role-playing simulations was established, it was a relatively simple step to extend the notion to another arena, in this case utilizing a more even mix of historical and contemporary figures. The Environmental Decisions Simulation, first offered in the Fall of 1988, starts with the premise that the World Bank has asked for an environmental impact statement concerning the building of a major, but hypothetical, dam in Zaire. The working committees are assigned different aspects of the report, e.g., economic, social, and ecological. In order to provide appropriate emphasis to the impact of the dam on Zaire itself, a technique similar to that used in the case of "private emissaries" in the Arab-Israeli game was used. That is, a number of Role Profiles are entirely fictitious, emphasis being placed on highlighting the attributes of native Zaire citizens and leaders who can "speak for the people of Zaire."

One of the main differences between this game and the U. S. Constitutional Convention on the one hand, and the Arab-Israeli conflict simulation on the other, is that these two are played with what the Confer system calls *items* and *responses* as contrasted to *messages*. This means that an entry by a participant in the form of an *item* becomes a kind of organizing principle for an ensuing discussion. Whenever anyone wishes to speak to this issue it is done in the form of a *response*, and all *responses* are simply "attached" in sequence to the original item, allowing for a very orderly discussion of a wide range of topics (i.e., *items*). Thus the underlying power of Confer is utilized more directly in these exercises, while the carefully structured *message* system that was actually developed for the Arab-Israeli game tends to be used only in that exercise and a few other on-campus political science games.

Still another role-playing game has been developed in recent years, this being the biggest departure yet from the original "character-playing" games, the ones described so far. The three exercises presented above base their entire claim to being **simulations** on the simple facts that all players are urged to "stay in role" and that controllers are provided to help them do so. In those games there are no "models of reality" with which the students are to interact. The Metropolitan Area Growth Games added in the last two years, however, do have such a model.

Based on over twenty years of experience with the Community Land Use Game (CLUG), Professor Allan Feldt, of Michigan's College of Architecture and Urban Planning, provides students with the opportunity to develop a city's metropolitan area over a period of several decades, typically from about the 1920's to the 1990's.

CLUG is a "generic" game in the sense that it does not purport to simulate any particular city. Starting with Ann Arbor, Michigan, in 1987, Feldt has proceeded to "load" the CLUG model with data for particular cities, expanding his efforts to include Detroit and more recently Flint, Michigan (actually, the whole of Genessee County in which Flint is located). Students play the roles of representatives of parts of these cities as they make everything from investment decisions to political decisions affecting the development of their area and the surrounding areas. In this model the roles can be scattered around in different schools or, for that matter, all be located in one school, for the essential dynamic is to interact with Feldt's model, which resides on a personal computer and guides him and his assistants (all of whom may be thought of as a different type of "controller," albeit of a different type than in the games described earlier) as they provide feedback to the students on the consequences of their latest round of decisions.

A much more dramatic departure from the original kind of game offered by ICS is the **non-simulation** game developed by Prof. Layman Allen of The University of Michigan's Law School. In an off-shoot of Allen's pioneering work with face-to-face logic and mathematics games, in particular his game of Equations, teams of students within a particular classroom vie with similar teams elsewhere on the ICS network to find solutions to a particular kind of mathematics problem. The basic idea is to provide the set of competing teams with a set of "resources" (single digit numerals and operators such as +,-,x, /, etc., including symbols for exponentiation, roots, and logarithms) along with a "goal." The latter is simply a number which the participants are to "shoot for" by assembling sets of numerals and operators that equal that number. Each different solution is worth a point, but "different" is defined as meaning that no two expressions may be made up of the same resources, no matter what order in which they appear.

This structure has the effect of requiring students not only to know how to perform certain calculations when instructed to do so, but also they must recognize that it is relevant to perform those operations to solve this particular problem. Further, students are offered the chance to "do research" when they cannot think of any additional solutions by performing what can be thought of as a kind of "experiment." This involves placing constraints on the resources and seeing how this affects the total number of solutions that fall into various categories, i.e., the number of solutions using just 5 resources, just 7 resources, etc. Armed with this information, inferences can be drawn and additional solutions developed.

The game proceeds by having teams add their new solutions several times a week. They see everybody's solutions as they go along, but they only get points for solutions they submitted prior to the time when they saw those very solutions because they were contributed by another team. The complete scoring system also serves to adjust the value of solutions in response to a team's past performance in a fashion designed to keep all teams working at their best; that is, it "handicaps" the teams as they go. The net effect of the exercise is to offer students opportunities to hone their mathematical skills while participating in a problem-solving exercise that puts a premium on designing powerful experiments and then organizing and utilizing the resulting data.

Teachers' Responses

In January 1989, ICS embarked on a research project aimed at finding out what teachers using the Arab-Israeli Conflict, the U.S. Constitutional Convention, and the Environmental Decisions exercises thought of the program. The primary goal of the endeavor was to provide an accessible forum through which ICS facilitators could relate their experiences with the various exercises. The goal was to elicit information regarding concerns and problems needing to be addressed and, hopefully, to identify "selling points" for future use. Jeff Stanzler, a graduate student in education at The University of

Michigan, played a key role in conducting this research and analyzing the responses of the teachers.

The research was conducted over a period of three months, commencing with the mailing of questionnaires to 204 past and present facilitators. Telephone follow-up work began soon after, and continued into June. A small second mailing was also conducted, primarily targeted at overseas facilitators. The questionnaire itself was brief, consisting of twelve questions largely of a subjective nature. Seven of the questions were asked of all facilitators, while there were two sections, made up of five additional questions, which were each posed to half of the overall group (the membership of each half determined randomly). In the end, 165 responses were received, representing a response rate of approximately 81%.

The major logistics issue identified with some degree of frequency pertained to the difficulty involved in running ICS as an extra-curricular activity. What were the perceived negative consequences of ICS not having a place in the regular school day? Some said that it resulted in an amount of extra work large enough to discourage their future participation. More frequently cited, however, was conflict with students' other extra-curricular activities, which manifested itself in terms of either smaller numbers of simulation participants, or increased difficulty in finding acceptable group meeting times. Finally, some respondents felt their power and/or control was reduced because an extra-curricular item was accorded less value. In the words of one past facilitator: "I won't do it (ICS) unless I have control over it, and I don't have that control if it's an extra-curricular item."

In designing the questionnaire, one of the issues explicitly addressed was whether or not the ICS-related workload seemed justified in terms of the benefits reaped from participation. Respondents were asked to indicate their response to the following statement: "The enormity of the facilitator's workload outweighs the benefits derived from participating in ICS." One would expect that present facilitators would likely disagree with this statement, and that is indeed the case (54 out of 64 respondents responding to this item chose the "Disagree" or "Strongly Disagree" responses). However, a majority of past facilitators (43 out of 71 responding to the item) also disagreed or strongly disagreed with the above statement.

Another issue investigated was the facilitator's sense of his/her own acuity in projecting the relative success of any given student. Facilitators were asked to indicate their sentiment regarding this statement: "There is no predicting which students are most likely to excel in, or derive the greatest benefit from, ICS." Better than 70% of both the present and past facilitator groups indicated agreement or strong agreement with this statement. Many responses were similar to that of Mark Kelty, a high school teacher from Mexico City, Mexico: "One of the great things about this class is that the average, or even below average student sparks and sometimes changes his attitude about school in general." Another facilitator's experience has been that ICS-related "surprises" take a variety of forms: "Often, students who do not perform particularly well in 'normal' academic endeavors 'take off' with the simulation, and students who are very competent with test-taking, papers, note-taking, etc., feel insecure and frustrated due to the unpredictability of the simulation."

The chief concern expressed regarding the exercises themselves pinpointed the sometimes uneven level of participation among the various roles and countries. This was problematic for a number of reasons. First, if a given role is not being played actively, it can discourage another participant who has invested thought and emotion into concocting a message. To receive no response, or at best a delayed one, after a major investment of time is obviously very discouraging. Other teachers citing this problem reported a day-to-day uncertainty as to whether or not there would be work for the students. One teacher reported that his kids were "never sure whether or not there would be things to do on the computer on any given day" adding that this "threw the day out of kilter." Another reported that circumstances were often such that her kids "sat around and looked at one another" and that she had to have two lesson-plans prepared to handle such eventualities. Fourteen of our respondents articulated varying degrees of concern about this issue.

A small number of facilitators, primarily though not exclusively based in the middle-schools, raised concerns about the intellectual level of the exercises and preparatory materials. These facilitators felt that the role profiles, etc., were beyond the ken of their students, forcing those teachers to devote additional time to adapting the materials for classroom use. All of these facilitators remained positive about the simulation itself, though, some even volunteering their services to work on such an adaptation.

Indeed, the generally positive quality of the responses was a source of encouragement. But the effort was also aimed at finding out just how many of our past facilitators "went away mad." The assumption was that many schools were no longer participating for reasons not connected with their feelings for ICS (insufficient finances, for example), but it would be desirable to know the relative proportions involved. To that end, the responses of the 96 past facilitators were re-analyzed. Each of these respondents, based on an overall review of the way he or she had responded to individual items, was placed into one of four categories ("generally positive," "mixed response," "generally negative," and "neutral/no comments"), and one of a number of subcategories. Only 13 of the 96 respondents fell into the "generally negative" category, although six of these respondents saw their unsatisfactory experiences as attributable to factors not related to ICS. Only seven of these past facilitators could be said to have "gone away mad." In analyzing the balance of the responses from our past facilitators we made an unexpected but gratifying finding. Forty-four of these past participants indicated an unqualified interest in rejoining ICS. Twenty-eight of these simply said they thought that this would happen in the future. Sixteen of them expressed an interest in rejoining under changed circumstances such as improved access to computers or the opportunity to build a class around the simulation. It should be noted that no explicit questions were asked regarding potential future involvement with ICS. All of the above responses were given voluntarily.

The Future

Plans have been completed for offering three exercises that differ somewhat from anything offered to date, two at the secondary school level and one entirely at the collegiate level.

An International Poetry Guild will group high schools together for the purpose of writing and "publishing" poetry. Each participating school will select a theme for its Poetry Journal and proceed to select and publish poems from the other schools in the Guild on that theme. A basic tenet of the program is that each journal must consist of a fixed number of poems, typically three, from each school in that Guild before additional poems from any one school can be selected for publication. The idea is to put a premium on encouraging poems from individual schools rather than letting a particularly talented set of students in any one school dominate a journal. Students and staff at The University of Michigan will serve as "mentors" as contrasted to "controllers" in this exercise. This is the first example of an exercise that was designed explicitly at the initiative of a teacher in a school participating in the ICS system. An English teacher in a middle school had been helping social studies' teachers with the computer aspects of ICS, and asked if it would be possible to develop something of interest to his students, particularly in the area of poetry. The International Poetry Guild is the result of that inquiry.

A computer conference-based "panel discussion" on the subject of "the peaceful uses of space in the twenty-first century" is also now available. This will involve a panel of twelve professors from around the country, discussing with one another how space explorations may influence the future career opportunities for present high school students and the impact that various developments in space might have on people's lives, politically, economically, culturally, etc. The students in the participating high schools will have their own conference in which to discuss issues raised by the panelists. Students will have the choice of either entering comments that they themselves would like to make, or they may participate in a role-playing mode, taking on the role of any of twenty-four prominent figures who are, in effect, "in the audience" being addressed by the panelists. These figures are designed to represent an extremely diverse set of characters who are, figuratively, attending the conference to be educated about outer space.

The basic idea of mixing a panel discussion with role-playing can be extended to almost any topic, and consideration is being given to making such a format available to college students as well as pre-collegiate students. The guiding idea behind it is to help students see how representatives of a wide variety of academic disciplines bring the results of many years of thinking along particular disciplinary lines to bear on significant world problems. By so doing, the hope is that students **discuss** diversity.

Finally, there are a number of other exercises just going into the planning stage. One bears the tentative title "The Streets and Elites of Detroit," which will feature inner-city youth advising "controllers" about what life is really like on Detroit's streets, to be played by college students as well as students in non-urban secondary schools. Another, focusing on Europe in the Year 2010, is aimed at Advanced Placement language students, the goal being to run four parallel games, one each in French, German, Spanish, and English.

Still another set of exercises is under consideration, designed to provide smaller scale, shorter exercises featuring specific national problems such as "flag burning," "gun control," etc. These are being designed for single-school use, looking forward to the advent of computers configured into local area networks (LANs), but also available on a global scale with each school's LAN serving as a "node" on a larger network. The point is to continuously push the limits of what computers and telecommunications may offer educators.

ICS would also like to mount a systematic evaluation or assessment program in the near future. One possibility under consideration is to make a series of statements about the effectiveness of a particular exercise available to Team Facilitators. From such a compendium, individual teachers (that is, the Team Facilitators) could select statements that are congruent with the objectives they have in mind for their students, working under the constraints present in their setting. ICS headquarters would then format these for response via a conventional Likert-scale technique, asking students whether they agreed or disagreed with each of the statements chosen, and make that evaluation instrument available to the school in question. The central ICS staff would then analyze the results, informing Team Facilitators not only of what their students thought of the exercise, but also how their students compared to other Team Facilitators' students who were offered the same statements for their "agreement" assessment.

There are many other, more ambitious ideas for evaluating the efficacy of the overall system that would be attractive to undertake, but any such efforts, including the simple questionnaire technique just suggested, will require resources not now available. In the meantime, ICS is committed to continuing to listen to the many people who use the system and making additions and modifications based on that advice.

6

Empowering Educational Researchers on CompuServe and BITNET

Jean W. Pierce

Two networks have been developed to address the needs of educational researchers; one is on the CompuServe Information Service and the other is on BITNET. They are very different systems, serving separate audiences in distinct ways.

The Educational Research Forum on CompuServe

The Educational Research Forum was started on CompuServe in October 1982. It was initially intended primarily for use by members of the Mid-Western Educational Research Association. CompuServe has been a nation-wide computer network, so people throughout the country began visiting the Forum. Very few members of the Mid-Western Association became members within the first two years. In 1985, the American Educational Research Association (AERA) took over sponsorship of the Forum when they hired a staff member who would upload announcements of employment opportunities as well as information from Washington about grant competitions, publications, hearings, and other matters of concern to educational researchers. Shortly afterwards, the Office of Educational Research and Improvement (OERI) in Washington started uploading information, as well.

127

The basic functions of the Forum have stayed constant through the years. There are three functions served by any Forum on CompuServe: the public or private exchange of messages, the organization of articles in databases called Libraries, and on-line communication through the Conference area.

Messages

Messages are organized in 17 sections, most of which are named to correspond to AERA's divisions. When members choose to look at messages, they are prompted to select a section. Within a section, they are shown a list of message subjects and the number of messages in a thread related to that subject. They can read and respond to any message or thread of messages. The sections are as follows:

0. Miscellaneous/Help
1. Administration/Educational Finance
2. Curricular Studies
3. Learning/Instruction
4. Measurement/Methods
5. Counseling/Development
6. History
7. Social Context of Education
8. School Evaluation/Development
9. Education in the Professions
10. Postsecondary Education
11. Teacher Education
12. Distance Education
13. Government-Professional Liaison
14. Employment Advertisements
15. Early Childhood
16. Special Education

Examples illustrate some of the uses of messaging. Within the Early Childhood section, one message on the Forum recently asked for leads about sites where a researcher could observe language development in low income populations with low English skills. There were at least nine comments in that thread.

In Learning/Instruction, a message asking about promising educational practices for a national publication received two direct responses and began a chain of seven messages.

Also in Learning/Instruction, a Parent-Teacher Association president asked for research about ability grouping to assist a principal and staff in decision-making. She was given a toll-free number of OERI in a response.

In the Special Education section, researchers discussed their mutual interest in using computers with special needs populations, among other topics. There are about 250 messages on the Forum at a time.

Libraries

There are 17 libraries, labeled the same way as the messages. Some files, in fact, archive past threads of messages that were of general interest (e.g., a discussion about where to find studies comparing effects of traditional junior highs and middle schools). Other files contain 1) discussions of research or issues of interest to researchers; 2) reviews, comparisons, and contrasts (of statistical packages, of readability formulae, etc.); 3) informative lists (e.g., a list of college courses offered on computer networks); 4) public-domain software for use in research or in the classroom; 5) drafts of papers by researchers who want feedback as they formulate their ideas (e.g., a discussion of the regular education initiative); 6) papers related to online conferences (e.g., transcripts of conferences, or a computer literacy curriculum that was mentioned in one of the conferences); 7) Washington updates— uploaded by AERA's Government-Professional Liaison (GPL) or by OERI; 8) announce-

ments of employment opportunities; 9) announcements of workshops or conventions; and 10) research summaries submitted by
OERI (on topics such as teacher incentives, at-risk learners, and
discipline).

Files can be downloaded from the Forum to a disk and read
off-line, or they can be read on-line. Libraries can be searched
according to keywords and/or according to the dates of articles.

Conference Rooms

Conference rooms are for on-line discussions with other
Forum members who are logged on at the same time. Typed
comments are flashed on the screen line-by-line. Public or private
discussions may take place in 17 rooms that correspond to the same
sections designated for messages and for libraries.

Conferences have been of three types: 1) informal discussions with anyone who is logged on — typically on Wednesday
evenings at 10 pm EST, 2) meetings of a committee with members
living far apart from each other, or 3) formal question-and-answer
discussions with invited guests. Formal discussions have featured a
number of prominent educators. Most of these conference discuss-
ants uploaded papers into libraries prior to their conferences. Then
users of the Forum could read the paper and be prepared to ask
questions. Each of the conferences was saved in a file for Forum
members to read later. One of the most successful conferences was
a discussion of student-generated databases, including teachers and
researchers conducting studies about the topic. Each of the participants had been a regular user of CompuServe and was familiar with
conferencing. One of the least successful uses of on-line conferencing was by committee members holding a planning meeting.
Most of these people had not been using the system prior to the
conference.

Objectives and Assessment

The major purpose of the Forum has always been to facilitate communication among researchers who want to: 1) share and compare findings about education, and 2) communicate with consumers of research—teachers, administrators, and parents.

These objectives can be assessed in a variety of ways. It is worthwhile to note that the Forum has lasted for almost a decade on a major network that has had heavy demands from other groups wanting to use the space. CompuServe is the world's largest online information service, with over 500,000 users.

Educational researchers have used the system. Between August 1988 and August 1989, people spent over 2800 hours visiting the Forum. During a seven year period, 492 people registered their interests in the membership directory. Three hundred ninety-five listed interests relevant to education and research. Many other people who visit the Forum fail to list their interests.

Educational researchers have been able to communicate with consumers of research on the Forum. For example, in the summer of 1989, there were 51 message threads, each involving at least 1 response to a message. Researchers participated in 28 of these discussions. Teachers participated in 12 of them. Students communicated in 11 of them, and parents sent messages in three threads. The most actively used sections (besides "miscellaneous") have been Learning/Instruction, Special Education, and Early Childhood.

Researchers have shared a variety of findings and ideas about education. By 1990, there were more than 175 files in the libraries, with an average length of 8574 words. The government-professional liaison library had the most files followed by learning and instruction and by measurement and methods. Most of the files have stayed on the system since they were uploaded, but there is a rapid turnover of files and the employment advertisement libraries, where timeliness is an issue.

How the Forum Has Empowered Researchers

Educational researchers have benefitted from the Forum in several ways. First, some researchers have met others with similar interests. This has occurred when one researcher read a message or a file left by another or when one used a keyword to search through the membership directory, or when both attended an on-line conference. Second, two professors who were located across the country from each other collaborated on writing an article, exchanging drafts of the paper at a fraction of the cost of express mail. Third, other researchers have found additional resources—leads about research in progress, reports of findings prior to their presentation in more conventional channels. Fourth, doctoral students have discovered a wealth of information. For instance, one student of policy studies received valuable advice from an expert researcher and evaluator in Toronto and also from a member of the US government accounting office in Washington. The chances are remote that the student would have connected with those patient and knowledgeable mentors in any other way.

This Forum on CompuServe is serving a useful function and has compelling reasons to be continued. First, only through a network such as can be found on CompuServe can educational researchers communicate easily with teachers, administrators, and parents. Second, at least one-third of the association's members are not affiliated with universities that subscribe to any other international network, and they should have an easily-accessible general network.

Other Benefits of Being on CompuServe

In addition to the Educational Research Forum, CompuServe offers a variety of other resources for educators: 1) the Education Forum is aimed at teachers who exchange messages about methods and materials they have used. Sections are devoted to discussions of educational software, media, the creative arts, social studies, sex education, home alternative education, etc.; 2) the Science and Math Forum provides hundreds of software programs and ideas for safe experiments. In addition, the forum fosters communication between science educators and scientists; 3) the Artificial Intelligence Forum is devoted to discussions of expert systems; 4) the Foreign Language Forum has a section devoted to Bilingual education; 5) a variety of forums are devoted to needs of people who own various types of computer hardware or software; and 6) finally, an information retrieval system called "IQUEST" provides access to ERIC, DIALOG, and other databases of interest to educators and educational researchers.

The Educational Research List on BITNET

In addition to the range of services available on CompuServe, AERA's university-based members asked for a special interest area on BITNET. That network is accessed by many universities throughout the world, most of which let faculty members use it free of charge. Consequently, BITNET has been the network of choice for most university-based educational researchers who use electronic mail for sending private messages. So in the fall of 1988, AERA created the Educational Research List on BITNET. It was begun for the primary purpose of disseminating news from Washington, so it was not interactive. The intention was that if enough members started using it and wanted it to be interactive, the nature of the list would change. Until then, any subscriber who wants to announce a meeting, request research-related information, or seek feedback for an idea can submit a message to the list, and any subscriber can respond directly to the sender.

Files that have been sent through the Educational Research List have included a description of the proposed OERI budget (and a request for comments on the budget), an announcement of public hearings prior to opening recompetition for OERI's laboratories, announcements of conventions and journals, and requests for field readers. In addition, there have been a series of requests for proposals, concerning projects such as 1) computer laboratories for colleges of education, 2) vocational education training and demonstration programs, 3) gifted and talented education training and demonstration programs, and 4) research and training in special education programs. Finally, the list has announced a number of employment opportunities, which have been sent to AERA by universities, other associations, government agencies, and school districts seeking researchers trained in psychometrics, statistics, educational administration, and other related areas.

Objective and Assessment

The primary objective at first has been the timely dissemination of news from Washington and employment opportunities that are relevant for university-based educational researchers.

The network is reaching university-based educational researchers. Some of the subscribers live outside the United States. And many of the respondents reported sharing AERA's messages with their colleagues. Over 1100 additional people have seen messages sent through the list.

How the List Has Empowered Researchers

The list has empowered researchers in at least two ways, according to comments made by the respondents. One of AERA's members volunteered, "I know for a fact that the announcements pertaining to Request for Proposals (RFP's) have resulted in faculty getting together, requesting the full RFP, and responding to it. So the research list has been widely circulated here, and is perceived to be of great value." A second List subscriber agreed, "an RFP announced by the system is now being pursued by our Dean in the School of Education and Professional Studies." Another reported,

"I have found the Educational Research List very helpful and informative. I have shared several of the announcements with colleagues—especially those relating to grant announcements. The Educational Research List has also provided me with information about avenues for professional development."

Other Benefits of Being on BITNET

The most common use of BITNET is the private exchange of messages and files among faculty members of different universities. But a number of other lists exist on the system, some of which are of interest to educational researchers. The National Science Foundation sponsors an interactive list discussing policies and regulations for their grants. There is also an artificial intelligence list. Psychologists can select to receive a list which is an electronic journal.

Differences Between the Networks

Educational researchers choose to use the Forum on CompuServe and the List on BITNET for different reasons. Since CompuServe is the largest network, it is very "user-friendly." It is menu-driven, and the choices are clear. The Forum is flexible, offering many opportunities for communication. In addition, information is clearly organized on the Forum. Members survey the contents which are stored there and pick and choose what to read and respond to. The List began as basically a one-way dissemination of information to educational researchers, with no opportunities for public or group discussion. Subscribers to a BITNET list receive everything sent over the list in their mailboxes. Information is not subdivided in terms of topic—nor is it separated by List. If they are not discriminating or if message subject headings are vague, researchers read all of the messages waiting for them in the chronological order in which they were posted. When they do that, they may find themselves reading messages of no interest to them, and the threads that do exist in some lists are disjointed—interrupted by messages concerning other topics.

Creating the Forum and the List

To start the Forum, it was necessary to convince CompuServe that a need and an audience existed. Since 1982, when other educational research groups have approached CompuServe requesting their own space on the system, they have been urged to use the Educational Research Forum.

Several times in the past, one or two leaders of a research group (e.g., a Special Interest Group or an AERA Division) have initiated plans for involving their board and/or members in use of the Forum. Each time, a section of the Forum was designated for their use. In each case, they found out that the members of their group resisted spending the time, effort, and money needed to log on. Perhaps their members would have been more accepting if the leaders of the organizations had done more to stimulate use by providing training in the use of basic commands, notifying members about message threads, library files, and conferences on the Forum, etc. Most recently, a group of distance education researchers has been funded by a grant, which will pay for their time on the system. This seems to be a more promising approach, for they have solved the monetary concern, and their members have demonstrated a commitment to using computer conferencng.

Other changes in the organization of the Forum have evolved from the interests of members who had previously joined the CompuServe System. Whenever several members have shared a common interest that did not seem to be captured by an AERA division title, sections have been designated for their use. This was how the Early Childhood and the Special Education sections were begun. This motivation for change has been effective, since the educational researchers who were requesting recognition had already been dedicated CompuServe users. Both of these sections have been steadily used since they were created. Once again, the potential of the system has been reached more fully by people who had, on their own, already made a commitment to use the network—as opposed to people who merely logged on at the request of an organization. On the other hand, it was relatively easy to start a list on BITNET. That simply involved finding a contact person at a university which had a node that permitted them to send out lists. For the Educational Research List, messages are sent to subscribers through a "listserver" node at Tulane University. The listserver manages subscriptions and record-keeping for the list.

Possible Uses in the Future

The Forum on CompuServe has enormous potential for enabling researchers to communicate with educational decision-makers and policy-makers. In the past, there have been informal exchanges on topics of mutual interest, but more could be done. For instance, the Forum could promote collaborative research by researchers and teachers. Frequently, it appears that schools are making decisions in the absence of research. And yet, there have been a number of exciting findings about how teachers can teach so that their students learn effectively. These findings have profound implications for restructuring the schools. If teams of researchers and schools work together, teachers and administrators could implement studies for researchers and the researchers could act as resources for educational decision-making.

The List on BITNET

Of course, researchers also need to communicate among themselves. And there are ways in which the Educational Research List on BITNET could facilitate communication among university-based researchers. The list could do more to promote collaborative research among professors at different universities. Research groups could form among subscribers to the List who combine their different perspectives to address problems of common interest. When they need to communicate privately, they could send multiple copies of electronic mail messages through BITNET. Using the List to create research groups could be very effective, for a variety of researchers subscribe to it. Most educational researchers are specialized in a particular field of study. They are experts in that area, but they may be unaware of related theories and studies in other areas. When they pose a problem on the List, researchers with different types of expertise are likely to respond. This could substantially enhance communication among researchers.

Conclusion

As more educational researchers use the Forum on CompuServe and the List on BITNET, both systems will become more dynamic. In the past, networks were hampered by a "Catch-22": researchers would not participate unless they knew that enough others were already using the system so that it would be worth their effort. Now people are starting to realize the potential of these systems. The pioneers have found what works and what needs to be worked on. Electronic networking is here to stay. It is cost-effective. And researchers have recognized the need to collaborate with each other and with school personnel. What remains is for more researchers to join their colleagues in realizing the potential of the systems.

7

Computer Conferencing as a Support Mechanism
for Teacher-Researchers in Rural High Schools

Lawrence B. Friedman and James McCullough

During the 1988-1989 academic year, seven English teachers from seven rural high schools in the Upper Midwest formed and used a computer conference to support each other's classroom-based research. Their computer conference was part of a larger project in which the teachers collaborated with a staff member from the North Central Regional Educational Laboratory and a faculty member of the Bread Loaf School of English at Middlebury College to investigate strategies for supporting teacher-researchers in rural high schools. The study reported here examined quantitative and qualitative aspects of the teachers' use of the conference in the context of the larger project.

The Larger Project

The seven teachers in the project were enrolled in the summer M.A. program of the Bread Loaf School of English. They taught high school English courses at seven substantially different rural schools in five states. Enrollments in these schools ranged from 187 to 819. One was a K-12 grade range. Three were 7-12 and the remaining three were 9-12. Project activities began at Bread Loaf during the summer of 1988. Six of the seven teachers participated. (The seventh teacher was in Oxford, England, attending the Bread Loaf summer session there.) The teachers discussed the project informally among themselves and developed proposals for

139

research they would conduct in their classrooms during the 1988-1989 academic year. Topics of their research were these:

- gender effects in instruction and word processing
- student beliefs and attitudes about writing research papers
- effects of teacher authority on student writing processes
- strategies for improving the writing skills of less successful students
- the effects of writing for one's community on students' writing (two studies)
- the development of computer conference etiquette and conventions

The teachers also received varying amounts of training on using the computer conference over which they would be communicating during the academic year. Near the end of the summer session at Bread Loaf, the six teachers there met with the two project staff for two hours to discuss their proposals and review project plans for the academic year.

During the academic year, the primary vehicle through which the teachers could support each other's research was a computer conference. Teachers and project staff also met face-to-face three times during the academic year. Teachers' travel, room, and board were paid by the project. In October the seven teachers met in St. Louis, Missouri, and updated each other and the two project staff on their research and discussed use to that date of the computer conference. They met the second time in February, in Elmhurst, Illinois. Before the meeting, teachers had submitted progress reports on their research to the project staff and received extensive written comments through the mail. For five hours, project staff provided technical assistance to the six teachers who could attend the meeting. Two hours were devoted to a whole-group, formative evaluation of the project. The second hour focused on how to make the computer conference more useful. The third meeting was held in June, in Elmhurst, Illinois. Four of the teachers and the NCREL staff member spent seven hours on the summative evaluation of the project.

The Computer Conference

The teachers' computer conference was one conference among many on BreadNet, the computer network of the Bread Loaf School of English. The teachers and their students could participate in other BreadNet conferences as well as their own. The teachers also could send private notes to each other and others on BreadNet. The teachers had unlimited, no-cost access to the conference. Each of the seven teachers had, or had provided by Bread Loaf, an Apple computer, communications software, and a modem. Six of the seven had printers. One teacher, who was on leave during the academic year, served as a paid conference moderator. He visited each of the other teachers once during September to provide additional training on using the conference and to trouble-shoot software and hardware problems. In addition to participating in the conference conversation as a teacher-researcher, he was responsible for monitoring the health of the conversation and doing what he could to improve it. The two project staff did not participate in the conference. (Both had intended to participate but did not. It is quite likely that their participation would have altered the character of conference use because they were not teacher-researchers in rural high schools.)

One way to characterize computer conferences is to describe their goal structures. Two key dimensions of such descriptions are (1) the degree to which the goal structure is emergent as opposed to established, and (2) the specificity of the goal structure. The teachers' conference had one established goal, to support each other's research. However, the teachers could use the conference for other purposes. During the life of the conference, a second goal emerged, to support each other in general. The teachers helped each other address instructional issues in their classrooms, deal with school politics, and get over the winter blahs. Both the established and the emergent goals were relatively general. They were much more general than specific goals of computer conferencing, such as completing a task or solving a problem, though not as general as providing a forum for discussion of a particular topic.

The project also set goals related to the frequency and topics of notes on the computer conference. The frequency goal was to have each conference member put a note on the conference once a week. Initially, the topic goal was formulated as a two-to-one ratio between messages about the teachers' research and messages about the context of that research. Context was understood to include anything about their students, classes, schools, and communities that would help them understand their research and what it was like to be a teacher-researcher where they lived and worked. This goal proved untenable for two reasons. First, the teachers found the goal artificial. Their notes often addressed both their research and its context. Second, the teachers found that the goal made it difficult to focus on their research. At the February face-to-face meeting, the original topic goal was replaced with a strategy that added a weekly "seminar" on one teacher's research. The teacher would put a message on the conference about his/her research by Thursday. The others would respond to the message and the "focus" teacher would reply to their responses through Sunday.

Computer Conference Use

The conference officially started on September 24, 1988, and ran through June 15, 1989. The following characterization of how the teacher-researchers used the conference is based on their 293 public messages to each other between September 24, 1988, and May 1, 1989.

Frequency and Distribution of Messages

The conference moderator sent 163 of the 293 messages, about one per day. The six other teacher-researchers sent 13, 15, 17, 22, 25, and 67 messages, a frequency range of between one message every 11.6 days and one message every 2.4 days. Their messages were distributed over the days of the week as follows:

Monday	50
Tuesday	46
Wednesday	42
Thursday	43
Friday	29
Saturday	17
Sunday	66

Use of the conference increased throughout the year:

9/24 - 11/22	49 messages
11/23 - 2/13	82 messages
2/14 - 5/1	162 messages

What Was Said and How It Was Said

Messages ranged from two- or three-line "check-ins" to multi-page discussions of numerous topics. A content analysis of the messages was performed to determine what the teacher-researchers were talking about over the conference and how they were talking about it. The analysis categories were *post hoc*, emerging inductively from consideration of the first 100 notes followed by application of the categories to those notes and refinement.

What was said:

• Computer mechanics: References to the hardware and software aspects of using the computer conference, such as serial cards and telephone lines.

• Project mechanics: References to making the larger teacher-researcher project work, such as dates and locations of face-to-face meetings.

• Project other: All other references to the larger project, such as the value of the conference in relation to other demands on their time.

• Conference mechanics: References to aspects of the conference itself, such as downloading messages.

• Conference other: All other references to the conference, such as whose research will be the weekly focus.

• Research: References to the teachers' classroom research, such as data collection and analysis.

• Classes: References to their classes and students, such as instructional activities.

• School: References to school life outside their classrooms, such as relations with other faculty members and preparations for prom.

• Personal: References to the teachers themselves, such as their state of mind, engagements, and personal life.

• Other: References to other topics, such as educational issues and local politics.

How it was said:

• Questions: explicit or implicit queries for a reply from conference members.
• Requests: explicit or implicit queries for a thing from conference members, such as a collection of poems by students.
• Statements: assertions introducing or about a new conference topic.
• Replies: assertions in reply to a current question asked on the conference.
• Responses: assertions in reply to a non-current question asked on the conference.
• Check-ins: brief notices that the sender is still alive and part of the conference.

As the application of the categories to this note illustrates, the content analysis goes some way, but by no means all the way, toward capturing the topics and communicative acts in a note and the note's relation to the ongoing conference conversation. This appendix also illustrates that category assignments were not precise, but instead reflected the predominant communicative "flavor" of note segments.

Appendixes B and C show what the teacher researchers talked about and how they talked about it in the 293 notes they sent to each other. For example, 51 notes talked about computer mechanics, 40 of them once and 11 of them twice, for a total of 62 instances of talk about computer mechanics.

Appendix B indicates that the most frequently discussed topics on the computer conference were the teachers' research and their personal lives. The teachers also talked quite a bit about computer, project, and conference mechanics, and about the conference itself.

Appendix C indicates that the teachers preferred to make statements that were not connected to the previous conversation on the conference. However, they also asked numerous questions which were answered sooner (replies) or later (responses).

Characterizing Conference Use

The data on frequency and distribution of messages, on what the messages said, and on how the messages said it suggest that the computer conference enabled the teacher-researchers to communicate with each other. However, the relatively high frequency of computer and conference mechanics notes suggests that communication was not always trouble-free. Most of the computer mechanics notes and many of the conference mechanics notes were sent early in the conference's life, during its debugging period. Their communication developed from messages resembling postcards and letters in frequency into something closer to a conversation. The conversation was truly wide-ranging and somewhat incoherent, as long conversations tend to be. However, the incoherence suggested by the many statements not connected to topics in previous messages has a positive interpretation as well. The teachers felt comfortable enough with the conference and with each other to talk about what they wanted when they wanted. Finally, the preponderance of research and personal topics in the messages suggests that the teachers used the conference to support each other's research and each other, the two goals of the computer conference.

This characterization of the teachers' use of the computer conference as a conversation through which they could support each other and talk about what was on their minds is reinforced by assessment of the computer conference during the summative project evaluation meeting. The four teachers who were able to attend the meeting asserted that they received support for their research from each other. They felt that the weekly seminar format which focused on the research of one teacher at a time was particularly helpful. They went further; each described at least one key insight into his/her research or classroom practice that resulted from the conference conversation. They stated that the conversation, and on some occasions just the knowledge that they could connect to the conference, reduced feelings of isolation. Finally, the four admitted to guilty feelings when they had not at least checked in to the conversation in what felt like a long time to them.

During the summative project evaluation meeting, the teachers also discussed the development of the conference. They pointed out that the conference became a more transparent communications medium over time for them as individuals and as a group. Only one teacher, the conference moderator, was familiar with computer conferencing. So, at first, learning how to communicate over the conference unfortunately coincided with learning how to use the computer and conference for six of the teachers. Learning how to communicate over the conference continued after all the teachers were adept conference users. Each teacher continued to develop his/her own voice for communicating with the others over the conference. As teachers' comfort with the conference and with each other grew, their messages became stylistically more diverse and more recognizable. The conference moderator indicated that his dual role as moderator and teacher-researcher made it more difficult to develop his voice. He traced at least part of his difficulty to his concern about how the other teachers would interpret his messages; that is, how they could tell whether he was speaking as a teacher-researcher or as the conference moderator. The other teachers also stated that they had been concerned about misinterpretation of their messages and that there were misinterpretations that were resolved over the conference. The teachers reported that they developed a sensitivity to this problem over time and, when possible, took more care composing messages that they thought might be misunderstood.

In summary, the development of the conference was a two-fold process. One process, learning the computer and conference mechanics, was relatively straightforward. The conference became mechanically transparent relatively quickly. The other process, learning how to communicate over the conference, was much more difficult because it involved learning a new mode of discourse. This process continued for the life of the conference, resulting in the conference becoming an increasingly transparent medium of communication for the teachers.

A last topic at the project summative evaluation meeting was the fit between the computer conference and the larger project. Five conclusions were reached.

1. The face-to-face meetings were necessary, fulfilling project functions that would have been difficult if not impossible to fulfill over the conference. For instance, the technical assistance the teachers received on their research in February needed to be done face-to-face or at least orally.

2. The face-to-face meetings facilitated conference use. First, they fostered camaraderie in a way that the conference did not. It was suggested that this was because the meetings allowed the teachers to focus completely on the project. Second, the meetings were occasions on which the health of the conference could be discussed and decisions about its use made, such as the change to the weekly seminar format.

3. The conference was necessary, fulfilling project functions that would have been difficult if not impossible to fulfill at face-to-face meetings. The conference provided continuous access to peers teaching in similar contexts who were in some cases friends and in almost all cases friendly and supportive.

4. The conference facilitated face-to-face meetings. The conference kept the teachers up to date on each other's research and lives in and out of school. This minimized typical meeting start-up procedures and provided a shared knowledge base for the meeting. Therefore, the teachers and project staff could take up the meeting's business more quickly and more effectively.

5. The teachers' shared Bread Loaf experience facilitated the conference, the face-to-face meetings, and the project as a whole. As a result of their time at Bread Loaf, the teachers came to the project with similar "stances" toward pedagogy and research. The similarities provided a framework within which to conduct research and support each other.

Implications

This study indicates that the seven rural high school English teachers, separated from each other by hundreds of miles, supported each other's development as teacher-researchers and supported each other through the use of moderated, small-group computer conferencing. Their success suggests that this medium, at least when combined with appropriate, face-to-face activities, is a strategy that can be used to support the development of rural teachers as teacher-researchers in particular and the professional development of rural educators in general. A teacher develops the knowledge base and skills of a teacher-researcher through an iterative process of learning, practice, and feedback. Development is quickened when the teacher can work with other teachers who are engaged in the same process. Rural schools often are not places that support and nurture a teacher's development as a teacher-researcher. The remote locations and small sizes typical of rural schools create conditions in which the developmental process is impeded, if not thwarted. In many cases, a developing teacher-researcher in a rural school finds that s/he is going it alone, unable to examine his/her experience through the eyes of other developing teacher-researchers and unable to learn from their experiences. This study provides evidence that teachers in widely-separated rural schools can use computer conferencing to create a "place" where they can support the iterative, collegial process through which each develops as a teacher-researcher.

Most, if not all, professional development processes for teachers and administrators are iterative processes of learning, practice, and feedback that are better carried out with colleagues than alone. Rural schools, again because of conditions associated with their remote locations and small sizes, often are places where teachers' and administrators' professional development is a problematic undertaking. The results of this study would seem to warrant further exploration of computer conferencing as a professional development strategy for rural educators.

The study also captures a little of the conference's development and complexity, its place in the teachers' lives, and its relations to the larger project supporting their development as teacher-researchers. The picture that emerges and its inadequacies suggest how much more we must learn about computer conferencing as a strategy for supporting the development of teacher-researchers and education professionals in general. The picture points to at least five aspects of computer conferencing that need further investigation.

1. **Goal Structure.** Suppose the teacher-researchers' computer conference had a different goal, a different number of goals, or more specific goals? How would these differences, or others in the conference's goal structure, have affected conference use and its outcomes? In general, what relations hold among the goal structure of a professional development computer conference, its use, and its outcomes?

2. **Use Format.** Suppose the teachers and project staff had not developed the seminar format. Would the teachers have received as much feedback on their research as they did? Would the feedback

have been as useful? In general, what use formats are appropriate for a professional development conference? At what stage of conference development does a format become appropriate or inappropriate? What are the relations between goal structure and use format?

3. Conference Size. Suppose five more or two fewer teacher-researchers had used the computer conference. Would the increase have made the conference unwieldy? Would the decrease have meant that the conference did not reach critical mass for success? In general, how does the size of a professional development computer conference affect its utility? How does size interact with goal structure and use format?

4. Conference Moderator. Suppose the teacher-researcher conference did not have a moderator, or that its moderator was not a teacher-researcher. Suppose its moderator only logged on once every two weeks, or that some of the teacher-researchers did not like or respect the moderator. How would any of these differences have affected the conference's use and outcomes? In general, when is a professional development conference moderator necessary? What are the roles of the conference moderator and how should they be carried out? How should the roles of a moderator vary across different-sized professional development conferences with different goal structures and use formats?

5. Shared Stance. Suppose the teacher-researchers did not bring similar pedagogic and research perspectives to the computer conference. Suppose that their perspectives clashed. Would the teacher-researchers have used the conference as frequently? Would they have found it as useful? Would they have sent more private notes? In general, what and how much should professional development conference users have in common for them to support each other's professional development? Does the appropriate shared stance vary across moderated and unmoderated conferences of different sizes with different goal structures and use formats?

Conclusion

This study of a moderated computer conference for a small number of teacher-researchers in rural high schools contributes another case to the growing "what works" file on professional development computer conferencing. This experience also produces an array of critical questions for another file on what makes a professional development computer conference work. In other words, the study is more confirmation, if more were needed, of the potential of computer conferencing as a professional development strategy and of the long way to go before that potential is realized.

Appendix A Example of Interactions

To my NCREL friends,
(Personal Statements)
I will try to be less crabby and more concise in this note. I promise. Hey, Mike, it's great to see you on line! Hope to hear more from you in the coming months. And Doug, I've missed you, too. Your project sounds fabulous, and I'm sure "weary" is putting it lightly when you describe how you feel. If it really is taking such a toll on your scalp, perhaps we can get NCREL to fund a transplant. Just a thought.
CONTEXT
(Research Statements)
I got some very helpful feedback from Don on my research proposal and just sent out a revised version on Friday.
There really is a good fairy or something because just when I was feeling totally frantic about getting the revision done in time, the temperature dipped to 25 below zero with a 65 below zero windchill, so school was canceled on Friday which gave me all of the extra time I needed. Whew.
(Research Questions)
Since I'm new at this I-Search business, I have a couple of questions that I thought you could help with. Is it true that any topic goes? I have a couple of kids whose searches involve finding people whom they met and have lost touch with. I can see this as a valuable experience because something like that IS real life research...sort of...I've told them to go for it. Any input?
(Project Mechanics Statements)
I am looking forward to Chicago. Since we've really gotten going, I have tons of questions...and it will just be nice to see all of your smiling faces again.
(Class Reply)
Jamie, thanks for your offer to be a resource for my kids. I will definitely take you up on that. Hopefully we will be able to get another note off to you soon, and this time their questions will be more focused since they have all started their specific searches. By the way, thanks for your uplifting note.
(Project Mechanics Question)
Have a joyous week. See you on Sunday. HEY, does anyone know where we're staying, etc.? I had called Don and left a message for him to call me back with the name of our hotel and info regarding transportation from the airport, but I haven't heard from him. Anyone?

Signing off, "I still wish it were spring," Marlene.

Appendix B What Was Said on the Computer Conference

	Instances per note					*Total Notes/Instances*
	1	2	3	4	5	
Computer mechanics	40	11				51/62
Project mechanics	41	13	7	4	2	67/114
Project other	2					2/2
Conference mechanics	48	7	2			57/68
Conference other	47	5	1	1		54/64
Research	60	28	13	2	2	105/173
Classes	9	7	2			18/29
School	9					9/9
Personal	81	19	6			106/137
Other	15	3				18/21
				Total		487/679

Appendix C How Conference Members Talked to Each Other

	Instances per note						*Total Notes/Instances*
	1	2	3	4	5	6	
Questions	58	14					72/86
Requests	34	3					37/40
Statements	81	48	36	12	4	1	182/339
Replies	46	9	1				56/67
Responses	60	15	1				76/93
Check-ins	21						21/21
Total							444/646

8

Explicating Expert Opinion: A Case Study of a Computer Conferencing Delphi

Michael D. Waggoner

Problems in Explicating Expert Opinion

The explication of the opinion of a group of experts is a multifaceted, complex problem. There are questions about how experts form their opinions. What processes are involved with analyzing a question, the subsequent interaction with the knowledge base, and the development of the rationale underlying the resulting opinion? What do the processes involved in opinion formation suggest about the structure and process of questioning an expert? What do the responses to the query process mean and how can we be sure that they have considered pertinent data? What considerations come into play when an expert engages in the opinion formation process among his or her peers?

Addressing the Problems

Increasing sophistication in research design strategies, methodologies, and statistics has been developed over time to address some of these problems in the collection of data and to improve upon the interpretation of that data in *post hoc* analyses. Each of these techniques and methods has added additional tools for use in obtaining the best possible information from the interrogation of experts. One such method, the delphi technique, has evolved from the survey research tradition and was developed specifically to address the problems inherent in explicating expert opinion.

The delphi technique was originally developed by Norman Dalkey and Olaf Helmer at the Rand Corporation in the 1950s for the U.S. Air Force as a means of bringing expert opinion to bear in developing forecasting information. The technique consists of a series of intensive questionnaires to expert respondents interspersed with controlled feedback. The original technique involved individual contact with the expert through questionnaire or interview and avoided direct confrontation among the experts. The questions were designed to surface several elements of expertise: 1) the respondent's reasoning, 2) the factors he considers relevant, 3) his own estimate of the factors, and 4) the information regarding the kind of data he felt would enable him to arrive at a better appraisal, and therefore be more confident in his answer (Dalkey and Helmer, 1963).

A delphi survey has generally been characterized by three features: 1) anonymity among respondents, 2) interaction with controlled feedback, and 3) statistically expressed, consensus oriented group response or position. Over the intervening thirty years since its inception, a number of variations have been introduced on each of these features. Varying the level of anonymity has been the principal feature with which there has been the most experimentation.

The technique has been a pencil and paper exercise requiring considerable amounts of time in administration through the mails and in analysis and synthesis by the monitoring team. Generally, the expert respondents were asked to comment on the syntheses compiled from the previous round of responses. Their interaction was essentially bilateral between the individual and the delphi monitoring team.

Advances in computer technology, particularly in the area of computer-mediated communications, hold promise for further improvements in technique with regard to explicating expert opinion. Adaptation of the delphi method for use in a computer conferencing system may be one such promising technique. Computer conferencing uses computers connected by telephone lines to enable group discussion among geographically dispersed participants at times convenient to them.

Modified for an interactive computer conferencing environment, the adapted technique still may use the iterative rounds of questionnaires interspersed with controlled feedback to expert panelists. But, additionally, the computer conferencing medium enables the addition of anonymous interaction and discussion among the experts, a measure which may hold the principal promise for improving the quality of the information by providing the opportunity for clarification of unintended ambiguity and for the introduction of new information or alternative lines of reasoning into the discussion while it is going on.

Case Study of a Computer Conferencing Delphi

This case study examines such a technique for explicating expert opinion that combines the strengths of survey and interview research, represented in aspects of the delphi method, with the technology of group computer conferencing. The delphi method consists of a series of questionnaires interspersed with controlled feedback to a group anonymous to each other. This combination of technology and structured group process provides a new research tool capable of producing results that cannot be achieved in any other single medium.

This study hypothesizes expert behavior as it was intended to be produced by the design of the computer conferencing system. It then goes on to compare actual behavior to the hypotheses. Data used in this study derived from four sources: review of related literatures, data collected (both substantive comment and participant information) by the computer during the course of the computer conferencing delphi, questionnaire responses from expert panelists and selected project staff members, and field notes kept throughout the development and implementation process.

Context of the Case Study

An opportunity to implement a computer conferencing delphi came in the context of a larger project undertaken by a consortium of eight intermediate school districts (ISDs) in Michigan. (An intermediate school district is a regional educational agency that provides staff development and research and administrative services to its constituent districts. Its geographical borders generally correspond to those of the county in which it is located.) Forming a consortium, these ISDs proposed a study to examine the question, What will be the impacts of high technology on the content, delivery, and organization and administration of instruction (K-Adult) conducted by local and intermediate school districts over the next five years? The study contained three components: a statewide teleconference, a national delphi study, and a future scenarios workshop. The teleconference brought together a panel of three leading educators to raise salient issues pertinent to this study and to raise awareness among the audiences in Michigan who participated in the teleconference. The delphi study was intended to develop forecasting and planning data about a range of questions by explicating the opinion of a nationally distributed panel of experts on technology and education. And the future scenarios workshop was intended to use material developed by the delphi in the development of alternative scenarios from which and toward which Michigan educators could plan. Consortium staff invited the author to conduct the delphi in a computer conferencing environment to elicit the desired forecasting and planning information and to test its utility as a tool for possible future applications.

A Need for a Conceptual Framework

The implementation of a modified delphi methodology on a computer conferencing system has been cited as having potential for eliciting better information in a more efficient manner than other available techniques.

Linstone and Turoff, in *The Delphi Method*, presented the case for potentially useful applications of this technology, but intimated that the telecommunications technology was not in common enough use at the time of their writing in the early 1970s to expect applications to be undertaken.

In a book published in 1978 by Hiltz and Turoff, *The Network Nation*, the case was made again for the potential of the technology and methodology. The authors cited the advent of the first computer conferencing system as an attempt to computerize a delphi process involving twenty participants from around the country over a period of thirteen weeks (Turoff, 1972).

Kerr and Hiltz, in their 1982 book, *Computer-Mediated Communication Systems*, discussed experimentation with a variation of delphi conferencing, but noted that there had been few studies at that date and that this was an area that would benefit from further study.

In a review of research on computer-mediated communications, Kiesler, Siegel, and McGuire (1984) suggested that "The conceptual framework for studies of computer-mediated communication will develop mainly from studies of social process." Researchers have identified key factors that need to be taken into account when working with groups in a computer-mediated environment. These factors helped to inform the development and implementation of the computer conferencing delphi model.

Computer-Mediated Communications

The literature of computer-mediated communications derives from the experience of the 1950s and 1960s with user interface concerns involved in information retrieval in the library environment, and from research conducted in the use of computer-based communication systems ranging from electronic mail to conferencing systems. Studies have focused on factors affecting individual and group use of these systems and on applications of systems to administrative, teaching, and decision-making situations.

Bennett (1972) underscored the importance of attention to the user as the key component of interactive computer systems in an information retrieval environment. Any intended model for a system, he suggested, must attend to four components: 1) the task to be performed, 2) the user, 3) the terminal, and 4) the computer stored information content. In order to achieve the task at hand, a human engineering approach must be taken where trading off occurs between design possibilities, system capabilities, and human use capacity and alternatives.

Katter (1972) introduced the notion of a user's "line of credit" that is extended to a new system or task involving an interactive computer based system. During this period, the system must deliver the expected benefits before the patience of the user is exhausted. Within this "line of credit" period, Katter also suggests that the user passes through three stages of development in becoming acquainted with interactive systems: 1) uncertainty, during which he gains a comfort level about technical competence to effectively operate the system; 2) insight, at which point he sees the underlying systems and principles and sees how to apply the system to accomplish useful tasks; and 3) incorporation, the point at which the use of the system becomes second nature and part of normal work behavior. The first two stages, in connection with the "line of credit" notion, are particularly important in informing the development of the computer conferencing delphi system.

Kerr and Hiltz (1982) have identified categories and characteristics that affect use of computer communications systems considered from an individual perspective. They include general characteristics such as common demographic information that can help to explain or to amplify reasons for certain behaviors.

Characteristics of Individuals
That May Affect System Acceptance

A. Attitudinal variables
  1. Attitudes toward task
    a. Relative importance or priority
    b. Degree of liking or disliking the task
      (pleasant/unpleasant, challenging/boring,
      etc.)
  2. Attitudes toward media
    a. Attitudes toward computers in general
    b. Expectations about specific systems
      1) Anticipated usefulness
      2) Anticipated impacts upon productivity
      3) Anticipated difficulty of use
    c. Attitudes toward alternative media
      (telephones, letters, travel, etc.)
  3. Attitudes toward the group (liking, respect,
    whether members are an important reference
    group)
  4. Expectations about how system will affect
    relationships with the group
B. Skills and characteristics
  1. Personal communication skills
    a. Reading speed
    b. Typing speed
    c. Preference for speaking or writing
    d. General literacy (writing ability)
  2. Previous related experience
    a. Use of computers
    b. Use of computer terminals
    c. Use of other computer based

      3. Physical or intellectual disabilities
C. Demographic characteristics
      1. Age
      2. Sex
      3. Educational level
      4. Race, nationality, or subculture
D. Environmental variables
      1. Available resources, including secretarial support
      2. Position in the organization (or status in the informal group)
      3. Amount of pressure to use the system (from superiors and peers)
E. Psychological variables
      1. Personality characteristics (e.g., Myers-Briggs Type Indicators)
      2. Basic values (Parsonian pattern variables)

Attitudinal variables characterize the mental set that the individual will bring to the activity; they need to be anticipated and, as necessary, accommodated in order for the model to function properly. Motivations for participation will vary and early identification of incentives and establishment of mutual expectations will set the tone for the individual's participation.

Personal communication skills, previous pertinent experience with the technology, technique, and topic, or special physical or intellectual conditions that may require individual attention may be resources upon which one can draw or may be circumstances that require special emphasis in order for the individual to participate. Similarly, demographic, environmental, and psychological variables may provide important clues to how an individual may participate in a computer conferencing delphi. An analysis done in association with the other variables identified above and with other participant profiles may suggest individual and group strategies for producing productive engagement of the participants collected for a computer conferencing delphi.

Most of the categories of variables noted above will have the greatest forseeable impact upon the process, and they will be able to be addressed before the onset of the exercise. With respect to developing the computer conferencing delphi model, an individual must also be considered as a member of a group decision-making effort. Again, Kerr and Hiltz (1982) have elaborated factors that may affect group behavior in a computer-mediated communications environment.

Group and Access Factors That May Affect System Use

I. Group Factors
  A. Structure
    1. Size
    2. Degree of geographic dispersion
    3. Centralized versus decentralized control
    4. Pre-existing communication ties or network
  B. Leadership
    1. Style
    2. Level of effort or activity by the leader
  C. Cohesiveness
    1. Sociometric ties
      a. Have members met face to face?
      b. How many group members are known to each other before they begin communicating on the system?
      c. Have they worked together previously?
      d. Do they form cliques, have many "individualists," or are they an integrated group?

  2. Competitiveness
  3. Trust or openness among members
II. Selected Access Factors
 A. Terminal access
  1. Own versus shared versus no regular access
   in office
  2. Availability of terminal to take home
  3. Type of terminal (CRT versus hard copy;
   speed)
 B. Direct (hands on) versus indirect use

   Composition and commitment of the group to the task is
more important than size in a structured application of computer-
mediated communication. A small group of appropriately expert
people who are committed to make a process work will outweigh
the conventional wisdom of having a greater number of individuals
participating in order to help achieve a "critical mass" needed to
give momentum to an open ended conference.

   Pre-existing ties among participants is an important favor-
able variable for unstructured conferences, but for a structured
delphi application, this must be carefully monitored. Literature and
practice suggest that expert participants not know exactly who is
participating to avoid, as much as possible, the influence of status
and position of a particular group member. Computer software
allows masking of individual identity, so they may interact without
direct knowledge of who the other parties are. Leadership has been
cited as one of the most, if not the most important variable correlat-
ing with successful group computer conferencing. Kerr (1986)
researched the impact of leadership upon computer conferencing
and has identified attributes of "electronic leadership." The computer conference moderator is more egalitarian in style than authori-
tarian. Since it is easier for electronic group members to not
participate or attend than in the case with face-to-face group

members, a leadership style that is more warm, interpersonal, and facilitative is required to keep people involved. At the same time, the leadership must be clear and strong. Lack of strong leadership seems to be the leading cause of failure of electronic conferences. Kerr also found that considerable on-line time was required. Hiltz (1982) reported a similar finding in study that observed behavior in scientific groups. She found "an almost perfect rank order correlation between the leader's effort as measured by time on line and measures of the overall success of the group" (Hiltz, 1982, p. 188). While the amount of effort required varies by group, she estimated an average of thirty minutes per day is required for groups that are engaged. Additionally, the electronic leader must be technically competent; he or she must be conversant with the system features to facilitate the work of individuals, or the moderator must have immediate access to someone with that competence.

In a review of the research on computer-mediated communications from a social psychological perspective, Kiesler *et al.* (1984) identified key areas that require attention if groups are to be effective in an electronic medium. Given the unidimensional nature of this communication, through typewritten text only, there is an absence of regulating feedback through nonverbal cues that are present in face-to-face or even mediated groups that are using video or audio technologies. These potential inefficiencies must be anticipated and accommodated in order to move forward the work of the group. A positive side of this single dimension communication that relates to the above is that while there are no nonverbal cues, neither is there the influence of status and position, and the attendant possible domination of the group's work, that can occur in face-to-face groups. As long as true identities are masked, where this is important, the ideas speak for themselves. Domination of the discussion can still take place because the floor is open to any group member. Still, structure can be imposed to control this phenomenon as well. Part of the role of strong leadership is to facilitate the work of the group in this new environment where social norms are only now emerging. Interacting in a group without all the conventional means of communication requires etiquette and norms to replace the nod of the head or the empathetic smile.

Kiesler *et al.* conducted experiments to test hypotheses in the areas discussed above. The findings showed effects on communication efficiency, participation, and group choice. They found that electronic groups were as task oriented as face-to-face groups, but, because of the keyboard entry time, took more time. Regarding participation, they found that group members participated more equally in the electronic context than they did in face-to-face groups; and in a related finding, electronic group participants were more uninhibited in their remarks. Their findings regarding group choice were not conclusive. Although they did find a greater shift in group choice, they were not able to determine why. One possible explanation they offered supports Kerr's research presented above regarding leadership. They felt that lack of leadership allowed the group to wander to the detriment of the accomplishment of their task.

McCord (1985) cited similar conclusions in alternative media with similar characteristics. He studied the effects of mediated group decision making when audio or video technologies were used. He found that leadership was a problem in that it was slow to emerge in mediated groups due, in part, to the lack of conventional nonverbal clues. He also found that mediated groups showed evidence of relying more on quality of the ideas presented independent of the individual putting them forward, but in the end, did not perceive the ideas to be as attractive as coming from non- mediated groups. This latter finding was thought to be attributable to the fact that individuals value ideas more when they can associate them with a source they have learned to respect. And, heretofore, that respect has been developed in ways other than through electronic media.

Using Computer-Mediated Communications with Groups

A number of techniques have been developed in an attempt to mitigate negative or unproductive aspects of face-to-face group decision making. Selections from the literature of group process and decision making reviewed above elaborate the rationale behind these techniques and suggest strategies to incorporate in the use of computer conferencing with groups. The literature on computer-mediated communication identifies user characteristics and behaviors that must be accommodated in order to facilitate the productive functioning of a group in an electronic environment.

Attention to Individual and Group Characteristics

First, careful structuring of the flow of information about the overall process and the operation of the computer system—that attends to the user interface, human engineering considerations, and new user stages of development—will result in participation in and satisfaction with the process by the participant. Similarly, such careful structuring that takes into account and accommodates individual characteristics and group characteristics, specifically clarity of procedural description and encouraging a feeling of group cohesiveness, will result in participant satisfaction with the process and the outcome.

Narrowed Communication Channel

Second, the narrowed communication channel inherent in computer conferencing results in the masking of a participant's identity and nonverbal cues to the group, thereby enabling statements made to stand on their own merit. There is nothing inherent in this medium to mitigate groupthink or tunnel vision; specific interventions need to be designed to avert these tendencies.

Masked Interaction

Third, the masking of identities by the narrowed communication channel of computer conferencing enables the experts to interact directly. The original delphi technique had experts reacting to questionnaires, and subsequently to syntheses of iterations of questionnaires prepared by the monitoring team. The use of the computer conferencing delphi technique may be able to move the iteration process along more swiftly by having the experts interact directly rather than through the monitoring team. This should be accomplished without jeopardizing the quality of the comments through interjection of influence and status considerations that easily enter face-to-face deliberations. Also, it would mean that this interaction would result in a high degree of participant satisfaction that the issue was adequately explicated, since they dealt directly with each other rather than relying upon information filtered through the monitoring team.

Development of Rationale

Fourth, the consensus orientation of the original delphi technique was criticized for producing only assertions of the majority. The computer conferencing delphi collects a transcript of all opinions, whether in the majority or minority or whether representing consensus or dissensus. Consequently, the trace of the development of the rationale should be more apparent.

The Process

This review of the literature led to the development of a thirteen-step process to implement and test the efficacy of a computer conferencing delphi.

Step One: Pilot Study

It was thought that an actual implementation of the computer conferencing delphi could profit from a pilot test. The computer conferencing system selected was the Confer system, first developed at the University of Michigan by Dr. Robert Parnes. While a number of computer-mediated communication systems could be used for this purpose, Confer had been in use and refined at Michigan for a number of years and it required no modification for the intended use in this study.

This pilot experience was designed to identify potential problems in three areas: 1) technical problems in constructing the delphi in the computer conferencing format, 2) respondent problems in participating in the delphi over a computer conference, and, 3) technical problems with the delphi items themselves.

Learnings from the pilot resulted in key design decisions implemented in the actual conduct of the computer conferencing delphi. It provided valuable experience in implementing a delphi on a computer conferencing system. By identifying problems early and having time necessary to solve them, the development of the actual delphi was simplified and was virtually devoid of technical problems that detracted from the substance of the study.

Step Two: Selection of the Expert Participants

In the second step, a list of individuals who were willing to serve as expert respondents in the delphi study was provided by the project director. These people were selected for their expertise in assessing the impacts of technology upon the content, delivery and organization, and administration of K-Adult instruction. They had been contacted by telephone, and mention was made that there would be further contact from the administrator of the exercise.

Selection of the expert panelists was a critical step, since the quality of the outcome depended upon their participation. The person who was in charge of soliciting participation of expert panelists was himself very knowledgeable in technology and education, having worked, written, and read widely in the field for many years. As a consequence of his expertise, some of the best people available for this project were identified and solicited for their participation.

Step Three: Initial Contact with Experts by Exercise Administrator

This step brought the first contact with the experts by the delphi administrator. This contact was designed to accomplish three things: 1) establish contact between the exercise administrator and the experts as a basis for future communication; 2) provide them with two levels of information about the project—a) general information contained in the two paragraphs of the cover letter, and b) a more detailed description available in an enclosed reprinted article describing the overall project; and 3) engage them in a trigger exercise that would help bring them into the process in a familiar paper and pencil medium that begins to build commitment to continued participation while providing initial material for creating the first on-line delphi questionnaire.

Step Four: Second Contact with Experts

The fourth step involved a second mailing to the experts focusing on further explanation of the computer conferencing delphi with primary attention this time on the technology to be used as the principal communication and data collection medium. Enclosures included: 1) a description of a "classic" versus a "computer conferencing" delphi, 2) a proposed timeline, 3) four pages of specially developed documentation on how to access and use the system, 4) an illustration of what a discussion item might look like as it evolved, and 5) anonymous biographical sketches of the expert panelists. The biographical sketches were included, without real names or pseudonyms, to provide the individual participant with a sense of what kind of participant pool was engaging in this exercise. At the outset of the development of this system, it was realized that care must be taken to properly sequence both the communication with the experts and the activities in which we engaged them. It was crucial to avoid inundating them with too much information too quickly. At the same time, it was necessary to initiate activities that would assist in organizing the content of the delphi while familiarizing them with the computer conferencing medium that they were going to be using.

At this point in the implementation of the system, we were reasonably confident that the task was effectively communicated, that the system was adequately explained, and that the pool of participants perceived each other as appropriate people with whom to interact over these issues.

Step Five: Computer Communication Orientation

Step five of the implementation process began with the participants signing on to Confer and going through the orientation conference—PROJ:ORIENT. PROJ:ORIENT items were of three main types: 1) self-rating questions, 2) participant background questions, and 3) illustrative group discussion questions. The intent of this brief exercise was to provide participants with a preparatory experience with the Confer system in which they would encounter questions in a form similar to the actual delphi as well as gain familiarity with the interactive pseudonymous discussion feature to be used. Additionally, this exercise was used to conduct a self-rating by the individual experts regarding their estimate of their expertise in three areas of impacts of technology: 1) content of instruction, 2) delivery of instruction, and 3) organization and administration of instruction. This information was collected for later use in comparing responses and positions taken by the group. Since participation was incomplete at this point, similar questions were asked later on the post-delphi questionnaire.

Step Six: Preparation of Initial Questions

The sixth step began with analysis of the trigger question exercise and resulted in the development of the first set of questions. Suggestions for issues and topics to be addressed in delphi questions had been solicited from all interested parties in the overall project. A major source was the trigger exercise responses. Experts were asked to identify the three "most significant current technological trends or products which will influence K-12 education in the next five years." They also were asked to elaborate on the significance of each. Experts were asked to name "the three most significant implications (e.g., opportunities, problems, issues) which technological change will foster." The responses to these questions were combined with other suggestions and an initial list of thirty-five questions was prepared. An organizing principle used in arranging the questions was to cluster them according to one of three dimensions of interest to the study: content, delivery, and organization and administration of K-Adult education.

Experience had shown in the pilot test of this system described above that clustering questions according to some consistent organizing principle enabled the reader to give better sustained attention to his response by having a context in which to consider it.

Step Seven: The First Vote

This third mailing to the participants contained two enclosures and a copy of the online questionnaire: 1) an "Introduction to the Voting and Comment Process," and 2) an "Example of a Response to an Item."

In step seven in the process, experts registered their initial positions on each question. Again, given the participation rate (to be discussed in step eight) and the post delphi responses regarding clarity and usefulness of procedural explanation and system documentation, we considered the procedural and reference aids that accompanied the first set of questions to be a useful and necessary component of the system.

To this point, we had simply accomplished placing a questionnaire on line. The next steps of analysis and synthesis of responses and public, pseudonymous discussion in a computer-mediated medium would introduce the innovation into this process.

Step Eight: Vote One Analysis and Preparation of Synthesis

Step eight, analysis of the first vote, began with the end of the period allowed for voting and commenting. Sixteen expert participants had registered their positions in this first vote, three more than had participated in the orientation conference. The responses to all the items in PROJ:VOTE were "frozen."

A number of questions were open ended, while some others asked for a specific selection among options. In the latter case, there still was opportunity, and all participants were encouraged to add text in elaboration of their vote or position. Many did elaborate, and, as a result, there was a large number of responses containing text. Consequently, methods of handling that information were needed. A procedure for doing this was developed using microcomputer-based data base and statistical software.

Step Nine: The Discussion Phase

This step began with a fourth mailing to the expert participants. In addition to being provided with the syntheses, participants were advised that they could review the on-line verbatim responses in PROJ:VOTE. As mentioned above, two measures were taken to attempt to stimulate interaction in the discussion phase: 1) the explicit invitation to react to the syntheses, and 2) the use of lead-in questions related to the synthesis. The previously assigned pseudonyms came into use at this point. The discussion phase was the component of this model that made it unique from both the traditional delphi that allows no interaction among participants and from face-to-face or other technologically-mediated techniques (e.g., audio teleconferencing) that preserve some visual or voice .cues that can affect the discussion and decision process.

Step Ten: Preparation of Second Vote

Step ten of the implementation of this computer conferencing delphi involved preparing for the second vote. The expert group's position seemed quite clear on certain items from the first vote, so those items were not brought into the final vote. Some items from the first vote were elucidated or clarified in the discussion phase so as not to require further attention. Consequently, in preparing items for the second and final vote, only those items were included that were judged as potentially benefitting from a second anonymous vote. Nine items were included in this category; some were slightly modified and others were taken verbatim.

Step Eleven: Vote Two

In step eleven of the process the items were placed in the second voting conference called PROJ:VOTE2, and, at the same time, mailed to the expert participants. One significant occurrence discussed above bears reiteration at this point. At the time the final vote was to be taken, participants were advised of the availability of a $500 honorarium for those completing their overall participation by voting in this last phase. All eighteen eligible participants voted within a few days. This suggests that economic incentives may be one significant motivating factor to employ earlier in subsequent testing or use of this system. Considering that these individuals are experts in their field and are accustomed to being compensated for the use of their time and ideas, it should come as no surprise that economic compensation improves participation.

Step Twelve: Synthesis of Vote Two

This step involved synthesizing results of each PROJ:VOTE2 item into a separate finding. Each of these, taken with other findings prepared from consensus reached earlier in the process, combined to form the fourteen findings.

Step Thirteen: Post-Delphi Questionnaire

The concluding part of the development and implementation plan, step thirteen, was the construction of a questionnaire to be sent to the participating experts for their reflection upon the substantive outcome and the system used to elicit the information. A concluding set of comments reflected on the overall system and drew from questionnaire data, observation, and analysis of expert participation and field notes kept throughout the development, testing, and implementation process.

Summary of the Study and Findings

Participants in a computer conferencing delphi described in this study, who considered themselves to be among the top third of experts in the areas pertaining to the impacts of technology upon the content, delivery, and organization and administration of K-Adult instruction, held the following positions. (The means are relative to a five point scale, one being low and five being high, except where noted otherwise).

• They were quite satisfied (3.7) that the pool of expert participants was of sufficiently high quality to address the subject of the delphi.

• They were moderately satisfied (3.4) and confident (3.3) that the issues relating to the subject of the delphi were adequately identified and addressed.

• They assessed the actual effectiveness of the delphi in explicating expert opinion to be of moderate to quite high value (3.5), but assessed the potential effectiveness of this technique to be of great value (4.4).

• They thought that more often than not (4.0) the positions they took, whether in the majority or minority, were represented in the findings; however, they thought that they contributed slightly more to the process than they received (4.3 on a 7 point scale).

• They felt that the discussion phase made a moderate contribution (2.8) to the final position they took on a given issue.

It is clear that, while moderate satisfaction appears to characterize the participants' experiences with the process and the outcomes, a few of the results, and their attending lingering questions, indicate a less than ideal implementation of the system. Specifically, these questions remain: 1) Why did participants judge this experience to be less effective than its potential? Why did the discussion make only a moderate to nominal contribution to their final position? Why did they feel they contributed more than they received? The answers to these questions are interrelated and have much to do with the amount of participation by the experts. There was a high expectation for wide participation established when the mailing went out to the initially recruited thirty-five experts. A number of later comments made by telephone, letter, and question-naire indicated a disappointment in the few people who partici-pated compared to the large and varied number who had agreed to do so, but did not. Explanations for the conditions raised by the three questions flow from low participation and the admitted moderate to low priority (2.7) that those who did participate gave to this project. Perhaps the computer conferencing delphi could have come closer to achieving its potential had the participation rate been better. The contribution of the discussion phase to the finally held positions was moderate because, in part, the discussion was not as rich as it could have been had the participation been more substantial. And finally, because the discussion mix was not as rich as hoped, individuals felt they contributed slightly more than they learned from the experience.

Following the exercise a questionnaire was administered to the experts. Analyses of the responses to that questionnaire as well as other observational data produced these major findings:

• The perceived outcome quality is related to the perceived actual effectiveness of the system.

• There was an inverse relationship between the level of self-rating by the expert and the level of satisfaction expressed that the issues were adequately explicated. The elite group was less satisfied with the outcome quality than the non-elite group.

• The clarity with which the process to be followed is communicated is related to the level of satisfaction with the actual effectiveness of the process.

• The use of pseudonyms as a technique to mask identities of the participants made little difference with regard to their uninhibited expression of their opinion; in fact, it may have been a negative factor by being a distraction.

•There does not appear to be a relationship between frequency of participation and these variables: perceived actual effectiveness of the system, or perceived representation of individual's opinions in the findings of the exercise, or the perceived outcome quality of the exercise.

• The group found the potential for this system to be greater than was achieved in this particular case. This was so despite the fact that the group was quite satisfied with the other participants, that the process was clearly communicated, and that they were relatively comfortable with the medium (use of computers and terminals).

Relationships between several other variables of interest, suggested by the research literature and experience, could not be conclusively demonstrated in this study. But these inconclusive findings, taken with those of significance identified above, do have implications for the conceptual framework developed for this study as well as for future implementations of the system.

Implications for Conceptual Framework

The conceptual framework introduced earlier was drawn from the research literature and experience; it contained four components: 1) attention to individual and group characteristics; 2) narrowed communication channel; 3) masked interaction; and 4) development of rationale. The experience of the exercise related above has implications for these components of the conceptual model.

Attention to Individual and Group Characteristics

Research and practice had indicated that this component of the framework was fundamentally important to accomplishing anything of significance in the exercise. Care in communication about the process and attention to users' differing stages of experience, interest, and expertise had to receive primary consideration before substantive questions could be addressed. The experience and analysis of the exercise thoroughly bore this out in both positive and negative respects. Positively, the process was clearly communicated and that satisfaction was shown to relate to the overall satisfaction with the exercise. Negatively, the excessive number of questions presented in the first round vote overloaded the participants and nearly proved detrimental to continuation of the exercise. Selected implications for practice are suggested by this experience and will be discussed below. But a review of this component of the framework suggested a correct reading of the literature and experience — care and attention to this aspect are the foundations that are essential prerequisites for successful use of this system.

Narrowed Communication Channel

Research and practice suggested that some of the negative features inherent in face-to-face group decision making would be eliminated in this new medium where the channel of communication was narrowed—stripped of the sometimes inhibiting nonverbal cues. The removal of these distractions did seem to take place. However, the lack of these cues, along with the delayed interaction inherent in this medium (typical in this electronic environment due to time passing between comments), may have been disrupting, since it was a decidedly different pattern of communication. As mentioned above, research was reported by Kerr, after the development of this system, that underscored the importance of leadership in electronic discussion. A designated discussion leader is one strategy among others that should have been more thoroughly considered. While the literature and experience suggested that distracting features of communication would be eliminated in this medium, it did not suggest what effects that would have on the behavior of the participants. This phenomenon is closely related to the next component of the framework, masked interaction.

Masked Interaction

The literature and experience had suggested that the narrowed communication channel should rid interactions of the conventional distraction of face-to-face situations. It was then inferred that if this more pure communication was introduced into the delphi process, perhaps better quality information would emerge, since experts could be interacting directly and not through the syntheses prepared by intermediaries. Though no claim may be made from this study about the superiority of information produced by this method compared to other methods, the evidence did support that this process was effective in producing satisfactory results. Consequently, this component of the framework seems to be conceptually viable, though more research is needed in this area.

Development of Rationale

The direct, though masked, interaction of the experts in a medium that collected their remarks in transcript fashion, provided an opportunity not available in the traditional delphi technique to trace the development of arguments or lines of thought. This component of the framework was borne out in the exercise by its usefulness in producing the content findings. The number of responses made in the discussion portion of this exercise was modest. While they were sufficient to lend credence to this notion embodied in the conceptual framework, it can be seen that more frequent, high quality interaction could create a richly developed, evolving commentary and analysis. It could provide a trace of expert thinking and reflection that cannot be captured in any other comparable form. The systematic observation and analyses of the exercise have implications for practice as well.

Implications for Practice

In addition to the implications for the conceptual framework deriving from the systematic observation and analyses done in this study, there are direct implications for future implementations of this system.

Clear and Consistent Communication

It is crucial that the communication with the participating experts be clear and direct from the outset. Although the process was judged in the end to be clearly communicated, the initial contact with the experts by the overall project director was not consistent with subsequent communication that came from the exercise administrator. One result was some confusion on the part of participants and the study administrator regarding mutual expectations.

In future implementations, securing the participation of the expert and establishing mutual expectations should be carefully undertaken, since it is clear that this process is an important part of making this system work effectively. At the initial time of contact, a number of important motivational factors should be assessed and expectations established. Among them are these: properly assessing the expert's expectations for the process, the priority that he/she will be giving to this among his/her other commitments, and the attitudinal factors that may affect participation.

Combine Trigger Exercise and Computer Orientation

Two technical aspects of the process may profitably be amended. First, the paper and pencil trigger exercise could be combined with the computer conferencing orientation experience. The orientation was conceived as a necessary component designed to provide some exposure to the system before participants were asked to make more serious use of it. By design, the orientation was less focused on the subject of the study. These precautions seemed unnecessary in retrospect. The open ended trigger exercise process placed in the conferencing system would appear to provide the necessary kind of exposure while moving the overall process along at the same time.

Reduce the Number of Initial Questions

The second technical aspect requiring change involves the number of items used in the votes, particularly the first vote. The number of items should be kept to under twenty and lower if possible. This was suggested by the delphi research literature, but was not heeded in this exercise. It is not reasonable to expect consistently high quality responses from the participants for an exercise of the length undertaken in this study. A few participants complained of being "overwhelmed" by the amount of material to which they were asked to react. Further, the ramifications of too many items for the discussion component of the exercise are serious. Unless some major synthesis of the first vote is done the discussion section becomes too unwieldy for the participants to manage.

Purposeful Discussion Leadership

Another major implication for implementation strategies comes out of these analyses; specifically, the use of an anonymous moderator in the discussion portion of the exercise. It seems that this function could serve two purposes: to facilitate the interaction of the group, as is helpful and necessary in face-to-face meetings, and also to provide, as needed, additional information requested by the group. Subsequent to the development and implementation of this system, Kerr (1986) reported research relating to the positive contribution that is made by a moderator in computer conferences.

Although use of a moderator had been considered in the original design of the system, it was thought that this might interfere with the interaction of the group. So in keeping with a conservative interpretation of the delphi technique, the decision was made to leave the group to interact only among themselves.

As reported earlier, there was an emergent leader in the discussion, who by virtue of his frequent, high quality participation accomplished part of this role. Use of this technique in subsequent implementations needs to be carefully orchestrated, because the use of this strategy could significantly influence the conduct of the exercise.

Special Purpose Grouping

Still another implication for strategies relates to a special homogeneous grouping of the experts by their narrower specialties. The delphi literature terms this a symmetrical panel as opposed to the assymmetrical panel which was used in this exercise. Using this technique, the phenomenon discussed above—the highest rated experts being most sharply critical of issues closest to their expertise—could be intentionally focused.

Future Directions for Research

The experience of this exercise answered several questions and in the process suggested several more. This concluding section of the study will address five areas where future research may be undertaken to elucidate relationships between processes and behaviors that surfaced in this exercise. The five areas are these: 1) frequency of participation variables; 2) use of discussion leadership; 3) real time conferencing; 4) special purpose groupings of expertise; and 5) attribution of ideas and their perceived quality.

Frequency of Participation

The findings of this study found no relationship between frequency of participation and any of the variables identified for analysis. Future research on system variables must address the frequency question. Since participants cited the lack of participation of their colleagues as a negative aspect of the exercise, it is important to know what variables influence participation. One strategy to address this would be to develop motivation measures that could be taken at the time of initial agreement to participate by the expert, and then relate them to his participation patterns as well as other individual characteristics.

Role of the Discussion Leader

Research reported subsequent to the conduct of this exercise underscored the importance of on-line leadership by someone with the designated responsibility of facilitating the work of a computer conference. In an open-ended discussion, the influence of this role is of less concern than in the context of a delphi-like process, since it is generally less structured. In the latter case, however, decisions need to be made about the role the discussion leader will play, since he may exercise significant influence over the outcome of the process by his actions. Future research should be organized to systematically plan for and observe the influence of the organizer on the process and outcome. Different roles should be identified, assumed, and analyzed; among these would be: referee of disputes, provider of data, interpreter, and facilitator through questioning. A comparison of intentionally employed approaches could be undertaken on questions that were of a similar nature to see if the approaches contributed to the exercise.

Real Time Anonymous Conferencing

One of the advantages of computer conferencing is that individuals may participate at their convenience, since the computer stores the information in its proper sequence and relationship to other questions and responses. There may be an advantage, however, in conducting at least a portion of the exercise in real time, that is, with all participants on-line at one time. This would, of course, considerably speed up the pace of interaction with a possible result of creating a momentum to sustain the discussion past this initial, real time phase. One direction for research would be to study the effects of using this strategy, especially with attention to patterns of participation subsequent to its use and relationships to participants' perceptions about its contribution to the effectiveness of the overall process.

Use of Symmetrical Panel

One of the significant findings of this study was that there was an inverse relationship between the self-ratings given by experts and their satisfaction with the outcome quality. This supported the preconception that the most expert participants would be most highly critical of the issues at hand. It seems that this phenomenon could be channeled to produce high quality results by employing an approach used with the traditional delphi called symmetrical paneling. This uses experts with a particularly narrow specialty, or who are otherwise homogeneous in a way that would contribute to the process, to address a particular topic. One direction for research is to study the use of this technique when used as a single approach, and when integrated into an exercise like the one in this study, to see if higher confidence ratings in the findings occur that are attributable to this strategy.

Attribution of Ideas

The last major direction for future research to be drawn from the observations and analyses in this study also relates to the role of attribution in the perceived quality of ideas. The design of the system discussed in this study permitted an intermediate level of attribution in two ways. First, brief biographical sketches were furnished to the participants in order to provide an idea of the backgrounds of their fellow participants. Second, pseudonyms were assigned to each participant so they could identify each other in the discussion section if they wished. The first appeared to be useful to the participants, but the second did not. And even with the uniform satisfaction with the participant pool, the participants perceived that they contributed more than they received. One inference may be that since the pool was judged to be quite satisfactory and the effectiveness of the system was satisfactory, the quality of the other responses must be perceived as low. The discussion earlier cited selected participant comments that pointed to conditions that may indirectly have contributed to the low rating given to perceived quality of the outcomes. What is not clear, of course, is why the comments were perceived to be of low quality.

One line of future research is to examine the relationship between attribution and perceived quality of ideas. The negative aspects of attribution were discussed in the review of the literature, but there is also a positive side to attribution—the side which provides context and lends credibility to the source of a position. One question for further research is this: What are the factors that determine the perceived quality of an idea? And a related question with a bearing on the system developed in this study is this: What are the conditions under which anonymous ideas may be considered as of high or higher quality than attributed ideas? Research on this and above questions could contribute significantly to the explication of expert opinion using computer-mediated communication systems.

Computer conferencing has emerged as a technology with potentially important uses. But characteristics of this technology require rethinking the ways to structure communication in order to effectively use the medium. While this study has only touched the surface in developing the understanding required, it is hoped that it has helped to lay the groundwork for further study in this area.

References

Following are selected references related to the problems of explicating expert opinion and the use of computer-mediated communications systems.

Bennett, J. L. (1972). The user interface in interactive systems. *Annual Review of Information Science Technology, 7*, ASIS Press.

Berger, J., Cohen, B. P., and Zelditch, M., Jr. (1973). Status characteristics and social interaction. In R.J. Office (Ed.), *Interpersonal behavior in small groups*. Englewood Cliffs, NJ: Prentice-Hall.

Berkowitz, L. (Ed.). (1978). *Group process*. New York: Academic Press.

Brown, B., and Helmer, O. (1964). Improving the reliability of estimates obtained from a consensus of experts. Rand-Corporation Paper.

Campbell, D. T., and Stanley, J. (1966). *Experimental and quasi-experimental designs for research*. Chicago: Rand-McNally.

Dalkey, N., and Helmer, O. (1963). An Experimental Application of the Delphi Method to the Use of Experts. *Management Science, 9*, 458-67.

Drake, W. D., Miller, R. L., and Schon, D. A. (1983). The study of community level nutrition interventions: An argument for reflection-in-action. *Human Systems Management, 4* (2).

Edinger, J. A., and Patterson, M. L. (1983). Nonverbal involvement and social control. *Psychological Bulletin, 93,* 30-56.

Glaser, B. G., and Strauss, A. L. (1967). *The discovery of grounded theory: Strategies for qualitative research.* New York: Aldine Publishing Company.

Hedberg, B. L. T., Nystrom, P. C., and Starbuck, W. H. (1982) Camping on seesaws: Prescriptions for a self-designing organization. *Administrative Science Quarterly, 21,* 41-65.

Helmer, O. (1964). Convergence of expert consensus through feedback. Rand Corporation Paper.

Helmer, O., and Gordon, T. (1964). Report on a long range forecasting study. Rand Corporation Paper.

Helmer, O., and Resher, N. (1959). On the epistemology of the inexact sciences. *Management Science, 6* (1).

Hiltz, S. R. (1982). The impact of a computerized conferencing system on the productivity of scientific research communities. *Behavior and Information Technology, 1* (2).

Hiltz, S. R., and Turoff, M. (1978). *The Network Nation.* Reading, MA: Addison-Wesley Publishing Company, Inc.

Hoffman, L. R. (1978). The group problem solving process. In L. Berkowitz (Ed.), *Group processes.* New York: Academic Press.

Janis, I. (1972). *Victims of groupthink.* New York: Academic Press.

Katter, R. V. (1972). On the on-line user of remote-access citation retrieval services. System Development Corporation. Santa Monica: California. Cited in John L. Bennett (Ed.), The user interface in interactive systems. *Annual review of information science technology*, 7, ASIS Press.

Katter, R. V., and McCarn, D. B. (1971). AIM-TWX: An experimental on-line bibliographic retrieval system. In Donald E. Walker (Ed.), *Interactive bibliographic search: The user/computer interface*. Montvale, New Jersey: AFIPS Press.

Katz, D., and Kahn, R. L. (1978). *The social psychology of organizations*. Second Edition. New York: John Wiley and Sons.

Kerr, E. B. (1986). Electronic leadership: A guide to moderating online conferences. *IEEE Transactions on Professional Communication*, PC-29 (1).

Kerr, E. B., and Hiltz, S. R. (1982). *Computer-mediated communication systems*. New York: Academic Press.

Kiesler, S., Siegel, J., and McGuire, T. (1984). Social psychological aspects of computer-mediated communication. *American Psychologist*.

Kraut, R. E., Lewis, S. H., and Swezey, L. W. (1982). Some functions of feedback in conversation. In H. Applegate and J. Sypher (Eds.), *Understanding interpersonal communications: Social, cognitive, and srategic process in children and adults*. Beverly Hills, CA: Sage.

Lewis, A. J., and Blalock, C. (1980). Computer conference on the future of education in Florida: Conference Report. University of Florida.

Linstone, H., and Turoff, M. (1975). *The delphi method: Techniques and applications.* Reading, MA: Addison-Wesley Advance Book Program, Inc.

Martino, J. P. (1983). Delphi. *Technological forecasting for decision making.* Second Edition. New York: North Holland.

McCord, S. A. (1985). Measures of participation, leadership and decision quality by participants in computer conferencing and nominal group technique decision making exercises. Unpublished Doctoral Dissertation, Wayne State University.

Office, R. J. (Ed.). (1973). *Interpersonal behavior in small groups.* Englewood Cliffs, NJ: Prentice-Hall.

Perry, S., and Kalberer, J. T. (1980). The NIH consensus development program and the assessment of health care technologies the first two years. *New England Journal of Medicine, 303,* 169-172.

Riggs, W. E. (1983). The delphi technique: An experimental evaluation. *Technological Forecasting and Social Change, 23,* 89-94.

Sackman, H. (1975). Delphi critique. *Expert opinion forecasting and group process.* Lexington, MA: D. C. Heath Books.

Tombaugh, J. W. (1984). Evaluation of an international scientific computer-based conference. *Journal of Social Issues, 40*(3).

Turoff, M. (1972). Delphi conferencing: Computer-based conferencing with anonymity. *Technological Forecasting and Social Change, 3.*

Van de Ven, A. H., and Delbecq, A. F. (1974). The effectiveness of nominal, delphi, and interacting group decision-making processes. *Academy of Management Journal, 17* (4).

Vinokur, A., Burnstein, E., Sechrest, L, and Wortman, P. M. (1985). Group decision making by experts: Field study panels evaluating medical technologies. *Journal of Personality and Social Psychology, 49* (1), 70-84.

Weaver, W. T. (1972). Delphi, a critical review. A research report. Syracuse University Research Corporation.

9

Computer Conferencing: The Causes for Delay

Donald P. McNeil

Almost a decade has passed since I first was exposed to the powers of computer conferencing. It seemed too good to be true to one who had spent most of his life devoted to distance learning. Suddenly — through the wizardry of computer electronics — you could talk to people across the hall or across the nation. You could interact with others at a time most convenient for you. But best of all, you could organize your work around subject matter topics which, in turn, kept your messages organized as well as dated and timed. And all messages went into a data base from which they could easily be retrieved.

Little did I foresee at the time the problems inherent in adapting this marvelous technology to the needs of faculty, students, staff, and administrators in American colleges and universities. The hardware and software were there, but the requisite attitudes and the will to understand, to accept, and to use computer conferencing were not.

My initial experiences with computer conferencing were as the creator and administrative head of the first American distance learning project that allowed students to complete all their university course work requirements by computer conferencing. As the project evolved, my staff and I quickly recognized the remarkable potential of this powerful new instructional tool, but over time we became increasingly frustrated as we saw the potential of computer conferencing for both on-campus and off-campus delivery of instruction going unrealized around the country.

But first, before the reasons for this academic "technology lag" can be fully appreciated, it is necessary to understand the numerous facets and nuances of this new communications tool as I discovered them during my early work with this software.

The Power and Promise of Computer Conferencing

When used either as a supplement to the classroom lectures or as the communications system for telecourses, computer conferencing impressed us with its ability to give everyone rapid feedback and to encourage lively discussions and a degree of involvement not often seen even in the classroom. These exchanges were between professor and students and among students themselves, and communications were always delivered and received at the time most convenient to the individual.

While messages in a conference were much easier to find than in electronic mail systems because they were numbered, dated, and timed, we could still write personal messages to anyone who was on the system and receive private replies from them as well. This was particularly important to faculty members and students if they wished to speak privately with each other. One could also send a message to the group belonging to the conference as well as designate additional names of one or more non-conference members to receive the same message.

It was not long before students in our distance learning courses were asking so many questions unrelated to the subject matter discipline being taught that we established separate topics for counseling students — such as in areas of financial aid, registration problems, textbook problems, study habits, even a small conference called "help" which was designed for the psychological and reinforcement support of the user.

Students joining a conference for the first time could return to the beginning of the conference and read all the numbered notes that had been transmitted up to that point in time. Often these new students just joining the conference found that their particular questions had already been answered by the professor, counselors, or other students in earlier notes exchanged at the beginning of the conference.

Students consistently reported to us that they were willing to ask more and to ask different kinds of questions on a computer than they could — or would — ask in a traditional classroom. While they still phrased their questions carefully on the computer, they were not as intimidated by the prospect of speaking up and voicing their own opinions in front of others on the computer as they were in the face-to-face classroom setting.

They also reported that because of its asynchronous nature, computer conferencing enabled them to review notes, read new messages, and write messages whenever it was convenient for them, and that this was one of the most important features of the delivery system.

Because all notes in the conferences were dated and timed, we knew that students were working at varied hours — some logged onto the computer in the early hours of the morning, some late in the evening after children had gone to bed, and several liked the time before breakfast to do their reading and writing.

Besides discovering its power as an instructional and coun-seling tool, we also discovered how much computer conferencing improved our effectiveness and productivity as administrators. We set up conferences by subject matter, by problem areas, by com-mittees, by administrative groups, and sometimes just between two of us to facilitate ongoing day-to-day communications about a variety of topics.

For example, as Provost of the program, I had a separate conference with my two top administrators, my entire staff, several with advisory committees, and a number of one-on-one conferences with other campus administrators, counselors, and faculty located throughout the university.

Similarly, my staff created conferences with the registrar, admissions office, the counseling service, office of veterans' affairs, and a number of other campus personnel with whom they often dealt. Even though my staff members were across the hall or in the vicinity (though some were miles away on another campus of the university), it was often easiest to type off a memo when it was on my mind and send it by computer without worrying about arranging a meeting or getting the person on the telephone (if it were to go to more than one person, that meant several phone calls). In other words, computer conferencing meant no more "telephone tag" — no more endless telephone calls to set up meetings — and it meant fewer meetings. The advantages of computer conferencing and organizing around topics with which one could associate in memory included easy retrieval by date, or name, or word string, which would trigger the computer's memory and bring forth long-forgotten details of messages we wrote or had read earlier in the week or month or even year.

Too often, I could remember only vaguely the nature of an exchange with staff members, but with a simple "find" command, I could retrieve the pertinent note or notes and be on top of the subject instantly. That retrieval feature alone made me a better administrator. Those of us who used computer conferencing regularly estimated that we increased our productivity by at least 25%. We could communicate with a great variety of people at our own convenience and with a single command. Conferencing meant no more relabeling computer addresses. It meant no more cumbersome and time-consuming getting in and out of electronic mail in order to read and write in the conference mode. And the "find" commands and sequentially-numbered notes stored in the data base made it easy for those of us with faulty memories to review materials.

We also found computer conferencing to be a very efficient tool with which to edit long papers or proposals where several people were needed to comment and critique. We simply created a conference with the name of the paper or proposal, invited those we wished to comment to join the conference, and began editing the paper collaboratively.

These longer papers transmitted to individuals and groups for group editing demonstrated another remarkable characteristic of computer conferencing. We could write the paper "off-line" on the word processor and "upload" it from the disk to the computer conferencing system. The receiver could "download" it from the computer conferencing system to his or her own disk — and printer — for review. The paper could be printed directly from the conferencing system or from the local disk. Thus, by sending the paper back and forth to several people at once, the author and critics could all see what the others were doing to the manuscript. And while one could send the paper to everyone in the conference, if someone outside the group needed to see a particular version of the draft, that person could be included in the editing process — as an outside individual — as well. Thus all the conference members and the "outside" individual would see the same draft version.

These uploading and downloading features are particularly important when long distance telephone charges are involved. Composing "on-line" over long distances is expensive. The ability to compose "off-line" and then transmit documents "on-line" in a matter of seconds or minutes rather than over hours of composition time is a tremendous cost advantage of this technology.

All conferences were private, confidential, and electronically secure. Nobody else could read the messages in a conference except those who had been invited to join that conference. The same was true of private messages: only the person addressed could read any particular individual message.

In our program, we had students from a dozen states, as well as one in France and four in Japan using computer conferencing to complete their degrees. Many were students who needed 12 to 30 hours in order to graduate. At the end of the first year of our program, six students were graduated — and because of the convenience of computer conferencing, most of them had never set foot on the campus. The interaction between staff and professors with these students had been entirely by telephone, by mail, and by computer conferencing. Almost all the students preferred the rapid response and personal attention of the professor over the traditional class-room lecture method.

In our program, for example, faculty became particularly challenged by this new instructional tool and responded to it with many new and creative teaching techniques. Professors created branch conferences from their main conference for the course; they then divided the students into teams letting them create their own sub-conferences to discuss various course subjects, returning later to the parent conference with their conclusions. Other professors created student polls, followed with a branch conference to discuss the results of the vote. Or they prepared short quizzes and gave assignments by computer conferencing. But the most lasting impact came from the freewheeling discussions that revolved around each topic established either by the professor or the students.

Related to faculty use of computer conferencing for teaching is the issue of ideal class size. Nobody yet has figured out the ideal size of a class being taught by computer conferencing. In those schools where there have been 10 to 20 students in a class, faculty members have complained of a huge workload the first semester. But then, during their second semester of teaching the same course by this method, they find that many of the same questions are being asked of them as were asked during the first semester.

From these early experiences, faculty learn to file their carefully prepared responses on the computer when they first prepare them during the first semester of computer conferencing teaching. That way they can bring them up on the screen the next time the same questions are asked in subsequent semesters. They simply modify and personalize the message and send it off to the second — or third or fourth — group, thereby saving time and effort. In other words, the learning curve for computer conferencing teaching appears to peak quickly during the first and second semester — regardless of class size — and tapers off sharply with experience.

Computer Conferencing Versus Academic Realities

While I now find myself even more excited about the potential of computer conferencing than I was during my initiation into the field in the early 1980s, my original predictions that this new system of communications would sweep across the academic world like wildfire were fantastically incorrect. The vision has so far lost out to academic reality. It has not been a wildfire, but more like a smoldering ash.

Why hasn't computer conferencing been adopted more widely and more quickly by the academic community? My experiences suggest there are five basic reasons:

Attitudes
Organization and Structures
Training and Support
Marketing
Costs

Attitudes

The most powerful force inhibiting the use of computer conferencing by faculty, administrators, and staff is fear. Fear of the computer; fear of their own technical inadequacy; fear of their colleagues' contempt. Many potential academic users have made up their minds that the computer simply will not help them in any way and they do not wish to be bothered with learning how to use it. But a large part of that attitude is based upon fear of the unknown or upon previous bad experiences with technologies either in the home or in the institution. In short, their "attitude" problem is more with the computer and all it stands for rather than with computer conferencing as a communications technique.

Faculty, administrators, and staff often are intimidated by the technical jargon of the computer experts or by the unintelligible prose style and ubiquitous but unexplained acronyms of the typical computer manual. Those who do step forward and learn to use the computer also unwittingly scare off their fellow colleagues with the zeal with which they flaunt their newly acquired "in group" technical language.

A number of faculty members harbor an unwarranted fear that if computer use becomes widespread in instruction, fewer faculty will be needed on the campus and therefore this imagined decline in employment demand might ultimately affect their own jobs. There is, however, no hard evidence that the computer ever has eliminated a single faculty position on the campus.

Another false fear arises from the classic "turf" issue concerning who is responsible for instruction on the campus. Many faculty fear that instructional programs and software prepared elsewhere — i.e., off the campus — might make them look bad by comparison. In fact, computer conferencing encourages exactly the opposite result. The professor remains in total command of the course and communicates with his or her students extemporaneously. The professor retains full control of the subject matter and how it is taught. Therefore, faculty need to be reassured that computer conferencing is a communications software tool — it is not an instructional software package.

If these generic fears of the computer — whatever the source — can be overcome, many more faculty members, administrators, and staff will become involved with the technology.

We know that change comes slowly in colleges and universities and we know that by and large the present generation of faculty and staff were trained in traditional methods. We know also that to overcome these attitudes we must devise different strategies and approaches to lure them into the world of technology. Computer conferencing, because of its immense and immediate benefits, is a good place to begin.

Before faculty, administrators, or staff members will commit themselves to trying out such a system as computer conferencing, they must be convinced that the new procedures will help them. Simple demonstrations can prove to them that they can improve the quality of their instruction, save time, or make their tasks easier.

There is no doubt that computer conferencing calls for a change in pedagogy. If a faculty member, for example, does not want to change from the traditional classroom lecture format to a system that offers even more interactive communications possibilities between professor and students and among students themselves, then there is indeed something to fear, namely that professor's indifference or hostility to the idea.

The same is true of the administrator or staff member. If people are irrevocably wedded to the status quo means of communicating — namely, the telephone, the mail, and face-to-face meetings — then no amount of persuasion or seduction will succeed in demonstrating to them the value of computer conferencing. As one president told me, "My system of communications has worked for years. Why would I want to go to all the trouble of learning how to deal with my staff and faculty differently? Besides, I'm not sure I want people to have that much access to me." The last sentence may say more about the president's real fears than the former.

As for instruction, computer conferencing calls for a high degree of involvement by both the professor and the students. It also calls for provocative, seminar-type discussions rather than the classroom lecture. Some professors cannot or will not make this change in instructional delivery format and its corresponding requirements. Yet almost all the experiments to date indicate that both students and faculty feel more involved in the learning process when using computer conferencing than they do using any other delivery system — including face-to-face classroom lectures. The feedback is positive, consistent, and very rapid. And constant reinforcement of the user promotes an intimacy and respect not often found in traditional classes.

Organization and Structures

In many colleges and universities, the computer center dominates and drives the technology life of the institution. Computer experts with their special argot and often condescending ways expect the average faculty or administrative staff member to understand almost as much as the expert. For many computer center "computer jocks," contending with ignorant or slow learning faculty, administrative staff, and students is a chore and a bore. In at least one institution, for example, the computer center refused to deal directly with students! All inquiries had to come through a professor — many of whom did not even know what questions to ask.

There are signs that these early demonstrations of arrogance are passing on the campus. Instruction manuals are becoming somewhat easier to read and are no longer dedicated exclusively to the "computer literate" alone. Special staff with superior communications skills and interpersonal sensitivities are being hired by the centers to deal with the "computer illiterate," those confused and frustrated people who dwell outside the technical world of computers.

But despite efforts of many institutions to centralize computer operations for reasons of efficiency, economy, and effectiveness, the very nature of colleges and universities makes these goals difficult to achieve. Academic and administrative departments often differ about their software and hardware requirements, about what kind of support system they need, and about who needs to be trained and by whom. In many institutions, an informal laissez-faire policy permits a variety of incompatible hardware and software systems to emerge and coexist like the variety of species in a zoo. This decentralization makes it difficult for something as interactive as computer conferencing to thrive in the academic zoo where so many species thrive.

In some institutions, several different conferencing systems are in operation (often without any one system knowing about the existence of the others). Moreover, an even greater problem is that computer conferencing, even when installed, often serves such a small proportion of the population. Usually, one professor or administrator introduces the system and it is subsequently used only within his or her particular circle of correspondents. Few people know that the same conferencing system can serve many other needs as well — instructional, counseling, or administrative — and handle hundreds of users in a variety of disciplines.

Training and Support

Of all the issues facing colleges and universities involved with technologies of any sort, training and support services are the most vital. It is amazing how many institutions and schools and states are willing to spend most of their time, effort, and money on hardware and software, and then such a disproportionately small amount of each on training and support. This is particularly true of computer conferencing.

Yet over and over again, we find that what makes a conferencing system bog down or dry up or just plain die on the vine is the lack of proper training and support. Several operating principles have emerged in recent years from trial and error experiments with computer conferencing.

First, at the beginning the training program often has to be one-on-one or one-on-two. For example, faculty often will not ask questions in front of peers; they need the privacy of a small session to ask what they deem to be the "dumb" questions.

In one of the first computer conferencing training sessions I ever attended, about 15 faculty members (many of them professionally distinguished in their fields) sat around listening to the presentations, but very few of them asked questions in the group. We even had assigned floating mentors to move from computer to computer during the training session, but still there seemed to be this terrible reserve on the part of faculty to participate openly.

Later, we realized that these distinguished faculty members were used to being viewed as authority figures — they were not used to being learners, especially in front of their peers. And thus, in this environment, they simply were not going to ask what they feared would be a "dumb" question about how the computer or the conferencing system worked.

Later, we discovered that when we offered one-on-one or one-on-two training sessions, the questions flowed more easily and the sessions were more successful.

Second, for many people, the trainer cannot begin at too low or too basic a level. The trainer must begin with the assumption that the learner knows nothing about a computer. This is true whether one is teaching a faculty member, an administrative staff member, or a student. I usually begin by pointing (with some humor, I hope) to a computer's electrical cord and explaining, "This is an electrical cord, and these two prongs are what goes into the wall..."

In training workshops with 10 or 15 people, one has to spend a good part of the first session convincing the people who are trying to learn that no question, absolutely no question is too "dumb" to ask. Usually, the new user will begin the question with something like, "Well, I know this is a dumb question..." "Hold it right there," I say, and then try to convince that person and the rest of the group that they must feel free to ask any question or else we are all in trouble. Additionally, the technical terms, the jargon, the nomenclature, must repeatedly be translated into simple terms until the learner gets some experience. Far too many people have been turned off to computer conferencing by trainers who have assumed the audience knew more than they really did. In some cases, the trainer must also help translate the manual.

Third, positive reinforcement is one of the most effective training techniques a trainer can use. Slow steps, reinforced at every juncture, continued practice, more reinforcement, and finally the learner will begin to experiment.

Fourth, support services are closely allied to staffing and training. Implicit in any full-scale computer conferencing operation is the importance of having full-time "trouble shooters" available to help faculty, staff, or students at any time within the work day. That calls for having technical experts available to answer questions about the modems, the telephone connections, the main operating system—just about anything that supports the conferencing system and that could be problematic or not work properly, making life difficult for the computer conferencing user. Some of these support services coincide with the training function, but unless this backup technical expertise is available in a timely and coherent fashion, the system will lose customers in the long run. Many institutions have installed computer conferencing systems only to wonder why the usage is so small; it's often because either the school did not train sufficient numbers of people properly in the beginning or did not provide the support system necessary to encourage participation throughout the duration of the course.

Institutional response to the issues of support services varies greatly. As noted above, I know of one college where the computer center will not deal with students; every request for help must come through a faculty or staff member. Another school I know has exactly the opposite policy. Not only will they serve everyone in the institution, but also if someone has trouble with the computer at home, the computer center staff will go to the home to fix the problem!

Part of the training and backup support for computer conferencing systems should involve the use of instructional technology. This is just a multisyllabic term referring to the technique of helping faculty learn how to use computer conferencing with maximum effect in the teaching-learning process. For example, when computer conferencing is going to be used in a course in conjunction with video courses, the instructional technology experts can help separate those parts of the course that best lend themselves to being taught by print, by video, and by interactive computer conferencing. When used in combination, these different means of communication can become a single powerful learning tool.

As some professors learn how to integrate computer conferencing with their courses, they can, in turn, teach others. In this case, providing released time for faculty to work on integrating technology into their courses is also a vital ingredient of a successful conferencing system. It not only provides the necessary course development time for the faculty, but it also acts as a reward system for those who become involved with technology.

Furthermore, using the more advanced students and interested administrative staff to help provide for technical support services — in addition to the instructional expertise of faculty— makes it possible to build a strong, comprehensive support system at a reasonable cost.

Finally, the issues of training and support services are all of a piece. When combined, they give an accurate measure of the extent of the institutional commitment to fully utilize and support computer conferencing programs.

Marketing

In a recent and potentially significant project at Montgomery Community College in Rockville, Maryland, we learned an unpleasant lesson. In 1988, The Fund for the Improvement of Postsecondary Education (FIPSE), an office of the U. S. Department of Education, funded a three-year experiment that will enable us to measure, compare, and contrast the academic and cost effectiveness of courses taught entirely by computer conferencing with the same courses taught in the traditional classroom lecture mode.

The design of the experiment required that the courses would be taught by the same teachers during the same semester, with one section being taught in a traditional lecture format and the other being taught completely through computer conferencing.

The professors were trained by us in the correct usage of the hardware and software and they adapted their courses and teaching techniques from lecture modes to student-teacher interaction by computer.

The College recruited students through traditional college marketing techniques — by placing special articles about the computer conferencing opportunities in all its college catalogs and related promotional mailings. We sat back and awaited the anticipated influx of enrollments. But not very many students came. It was embarrassing.

In analyzing our failure to recruit a satisfactory number of computer conferencing students, we realized that besides the fact that computer conferencing was a new "product" offering on the campus market, we had not marketed it well. We had been content with routine collegiate marketing announcements in traditional campus mailings. We had made the classic marketing mistake of using traditional marketing techniques to market a very nontraditional product to what we had also failed to recognize was probably going to be a nontraditional user market.

Montgomery County is a rapidly growing residential and commercial county just north of Washington, D.C., and it is one of the most affluent and upwardly mobile counties in the nation. Companies such as IBM and the Marriott Corporation are only two of a number of the Fortune 500 companies that either headquarter or have huge installations in the county. Furthermore, the College's main campus is located in the heart of this metropolitan area's largest "high tech" corridor. Computers, we knew, were located on most desks in most offices within a ten mile radius of the campus.

So in preparing for the second semester of our experiment, we completely revamped our marketing strategy to more closely fit our product. First, we carefully defined a number of target student audiences. Second, besides the standard notices and stories in the College's publications, we studied the demographics of our newly identified target markets in order to draw conclusions about the lifestyles of our potential students.

As a result of this research, we advertised in a regional magazine devoted to computer communications. We designed direct mailings for groups such as Parents Without Partners. We also sent direct mailings to all pre-registrants in the courses where computer conferencing was going to be offered. We sent a marketing letter to 175 corporate personnel officers. Direct mailings went out to a number of groups who work with and for the physically challenged adult community, a group we knew often had special difficulty commuting to the campus. We placed feature articles in the widely read Montgomery County neighborhood newspapers and advertised in both the *Washington Post* and the suburban Maryland daily newspaper.

One of the major marketing problems we discovered from analysis of our dismal first semester marketing efforts was that while many potential students had computers either at work or at home, precious few had modems or knew how to use a modem to communicate by computer, either through electronic mail or by computer conferencing. Consequently, for the second semester of the experiment, the College bought a number of modems for our students and we advertised in all of our marketing pieces that the modem — plus the training on how to use it — would be free to all enrolled students in our courses.

As a result of reorganizing our marketing according to a careful analysis of our projected student market segments and those students' lifestyles and needs, by registration day we had more than our minimum quota of enrolled computer conferencing students for each of the courses in our experiment.

Having learned our marketing lesson early, we anticipate that future enrollments will become even more impressive and that by the end of the FIPSE experiment we will be able to contribute important new knowledge to the solution of what has been one of the major stumbling blocks to the adoption of computer conferencing on the campus — namely, recruiting sufficient numbers of students to justify the investment by the institution.

Costs

Estimating costs for computer conferencing is an imperfect art. Doing so accurately depends on where you start. If the institution has no computers and one has to start from scratch, it can be very expensive. But today most institutions have computers, either at a person's desk or in a laboratory. Many institutions are now creating local area networks that tie computers together in an interactive mode. Many students and faculty are buying their own computers, and many working students have access to computers in the work place. All this, coupled with the continuing downward spiral of prices for computers and the necessary add-ons, means that the costs for adequate hardware and software are no longer out of reach for most people.

For computer conferencing, the institution does need the system software for whichever system will be used. Prices currently range from $3,000 to $25,000, with $10,000 being the average for a system that will handle large numbers of users. These costs, too, vary and will presumably decline in the coming years.

In addition to the computer, the individual user will need a modem to transmit the messages over the telephone line and communications software (to tell the modem how to do it). If all the users are in the same area, everyone will dial a local number for access. However, if students, for example, need to call long distance to reach the teacher, then there will be additional telephone line charges. There are several ways in which telephone line charges can be handled: First, each student can pay the long distance charges of their communications with the class. Second, the school can contract with a company that operates a computer conferencing system and pay the company on an hourly use basis, which can become expensive if no limits are placed on the "on line" time available to the student. The estimated or maximum allowable charges for the time each student will use the telephone lines during the course are usually built into the tuition.

In recent years, these phone line costs have decreased rapidly because of the computer's ability to "upload" and "download" messages to one's own disk, thus bypassing costly "online" time previously required to type out the message or to read it while "on-line." In other words, if messages are composed on the computer's word processor and "uploaded" into the computer conferencing mailboxes, only a couple of minutes of telephone time line charges are used. The same cost advantages accrue when the inbox of all the messages received by a user are "downloaded" to a local computer where the user reads them at leisure "off line." Obviously, these initial expenses and ongoing costs can restrain administrators, faculty, staff, and students from using computer conferencing. But costs even in the last decade have dropped dramatically and they promise to continue to do so.

Conclusion

Too often, institutions consider only hardware and software costs when considering conferencing systems. It is imperative that the school also calculate other related costs including that of training personnel, released time for faculty course development, and a support system that operates with the same hours that the library is open.

The most powerful argument for computer conferencing rests not on costs but on its ability to span distances both long and short, to empower the professor and students to interact with each other rapidly and extemporaneously, to gather around the electronic table those people who wish to participate, and, with single commands, communicate with everyone else in the group — each doing so at his or her own convenience. That is a power that we have not had until recently.

It may take longer than any of us thought for computer conferencing to be utilized the way we initially envisioned. Originally, distance learning was thought to be the primary target area for this new communications tool, and it is pretty clear that distance education will hold some sizable share of the market. But over time, the real expansion will come from successfully integrating computer conferencing with audio and video and print materials. The laser disc, fax machine, and audio and video recorders, along with the computer, will be used in combination with each other. And in those developing combinations, used either on campus or off campus, computer conferencing will play a significant role.

10

Empowering for Technological Change

Thomas J. Switzer

The single most important component in the effective use of educational technology is human decision-making. This assertion, although verging on the obvious, is frequently forgotten when dealing with things technological. Part of the problem is that so much of our lives these days is spent in dealing with technology that we tend to think of various technologies categorically. All technologies, it seems, share certain characteristics. A Rand Corporation study (1975) identified the following general attributes of a technology or product:

- clarity and specificity of goals
- specificity of treatment
- a clear relation between treatment and outcomes
- passive user involvement
- a high level of certainty of outcome
- a unitary adopter

A moment's reflection about our use of most technologies such as television, video cam recorders, microwave ovens, etc., confirms these characteristics. This same Rand study goes on to point out, however, that the general attributes of educational innovation are quite opposite. For educational innovations:

- treatments are incompletely specified
- outcomes are uncertain

- active user involvement is required
- the adopter is not unitary but a policy system or policy unit
- the relationship of project treatment to overall institutional goals is unclear or unspecified

In dealing with the use of technology in education, we have, of course, a merging of these attributes. Generally speaking, the technologies we use in education have the attributes identified in the Rand study. The technology will do what it purports to do with great degrees of certainty. It is in its application to issues in education where uncertainty occurs, where human decision-making, with all of its frailties, becomes far more important than the technology itself. It is in the educational arena where complicated issues of uncertain goals, uncertain applications, and issues of values and ethics come to the fore. Technology is, of course, neither intrinsically good nor bad, useful or not useful. The social inventions we create around the technologies are what makes a difference to humankind.

The key issues, then, in the proper utilization of educational technology involve human issues, not hardware issues. The social inventions we create in schools to make use of the technology, how we actually conceive of the use of the technology in teaching, are what makes the difference.

A Technological Wasteland

Arthur Bester once described education as a great wasteland. (Bester, 1985) To some people, this wasteland metaphor might aptly describe our past experiences in education with the use of technology. Instructional television, language laboratories, overhead projectors, and even microcomputers, although promising great potential for improving instruction and ultimately student learning, seem not to have lived up to their potential. This leads some critics of the use of technology in schools to conclude that technology has only a limited, perhaps insignificant, role to play in the nation's classrooms. This logic, however, misses the key factor of implementation. If these past efforts at the use of technology to improve education are examined carefully, it can just as easily be concluded that the technology did not fail and that the proposed uses for the technology were indeed appropriate. What failed was our inability to provide an implementation scheme to give the techno-logical innovations any reasonable chance to succeed within a complex social environment. Frequently, the concept or product that was being implemented never made it into the classroom in any form that gave it even a remote chance of being successful. Insuf-ficient equipment, lack of support staff, inadequate funding, limited staff development, and lack of administrative support are but a few of the many factors that determine the success or failure of an educational innovation. These factors have nothing to do with the basic conceptual design of the innovation itself. The problem, then, seems to be more with insufficient or inefficient implementation than with faulty product or concept design. Implementation is not everything to successful educational change, but it is close to it.

Change Literature

The body of literature dealing with the change process is only of limited help to us in understanding how best to implement educational technology. This is true for several reasons.

First, most of the literature on change and the change process has come from fields of study other than education (agricul-ture, medicine, business, etc.). Although there is some general-izability of findings from literature in these fields to education, the institution of education is sufficiently unique to make one cautious about relying too heavily on this literature. Knowing this literature base does, however, help one appreciate the uniqueness of bringing about change in educational settings.

Second, we are increasingly aware that how best to effect change is highly situation specific. It is possible, of course, to draw generalizations from fields such as organizational behavior that can apply, more or less, from one context to another. The reality is, however, that the particular context in which change is being implemented, with all of its history, power structures, norms and values, etc., suggests how one can best approach change in that social situation.

Third, we do not yet have a rich body of literature dealing with change in specific social context. As we have further acceptance of case study approaches, small research paradigms, phenomenological approaches, etc., to research, this body of literature is starting to develop (Bowden, 1988; Canning, 1988; Letscher, 1982; Poppard, 1982). We need, however, far more research of this type.

Some Practical Wisdom

Although one can learn a great deal from the research and writing of others, one can supplement that knowledge by in-depth reflection on one's direct previous experience. For the past ten years, the author has been fortunate, first at the University of Michigan and now at the University of Northern Iowa, to be in a position to support the use of technology in education, in particular the development and use of computer conferencing. Based on these experiences and on a longstanding academic interest in how change occurs in education, I make the following suggestions for consideration when implementing technology in education. Although the examples I will use are based heavily on computer conferencing, the generalizations, I believe, apply to a broad range of efforts to bring about the use of technology in education.

Develop a Vision

Not only is change in education highly context specific, but also the initiative for change frequently resides within the heart and mind of a particular individual. When that individual changes focus or moves on to another position, the initiative for that change within the organization is frequently lost. The change did not represent an institutional commitment. For change to have a long life and to eventually become ingrained into the fabric of the organization, it must be a component of a vision "shared" by members of the organization. Concerning computer conferencing, that vision might consist of a large network of educators being able to interact in a cost-effective manner without barriers of time and space in the pursuit of solutions to real educational problems. Inherent in the vision is, of course, a commitment to the value of such networking that is shared by numerous individuals within the organization.

Focus on a Theme

Focus on a theme that helps define the vision and that can be communicated to others. Several such themes can incorporate the use of computer conferencing. For example, with computer conferencing we might focus on the theme of collective intelligence. This theme focuses on the value of computer conferencing in allowing the collective intelligence of all of the participants in the conference to be brought to bear on an important issue. Another theme might be the knowledge base that exists in professional practice. Through the use of computer conferencing, we provide the mechanism for educational practitioners to bring the knowledge base they possess to bear on educational issues. Or we might develop the theme of graduation into the university and use computer conferencing to link to our alumni to provide them continuing professional support from the university. Another example would be the theme of the university as a receptacle of knowledge as well as a source of knowledge. This theme would focus on the use of computer conferencing as a mechanism for pouring information into the university instead of the usual perception of the university as a source of knowledge. The point here is that the theme gives definition to your vision and helps to communicate to others what you are trying to achieve through computer conferencing or other uses of technology.

Attack Real Educational Problems

Technology is neutral in the sense that a particular technology can be used for multiple purposes. The diversity of applications for the microcomputer is a good example of the technology being used to achieve multiple ends. What we choose to do with the technology is what makes a difference. Yet we seem to have few good models of the use of technology in education to help us deal with crucial, highly visible issues. We talk about the infusion of microcomputers into the curriculum or about the use of interactive video discs to enrich the curriculum, but these statements beg for more precise definition. What issues are we trying to solve? How do we give focus to these efforts?

Computer conferencing can again provide some examples. At the University of Northern Iowa we are concerned, as are educators throughout the country, about the limited number of minority youths who are entering the teaching profession. Traditional recruitment methods appear unsuccessful in attracting minority young people to teaching. To deal with this problem, we are implementing an early identification program where minority youths in five cooperating school districts, starting in the fifth and sixth grades, work with university and school personnel to prepare them for a career in teaching. These cohort groups of minority youths are provided specific experiences throughout their precollegiate education, for the four years of their teacher preparation program, and for the first three years of professional practice. Through the use of computer conferencing, these minority young people in various geographic locations around Iowa can be linked to each other and to the university in a cost-effective manner. The computer conferencing is seen not as a tangential aspect of this effort to bring minorities into teaching but is seen as an integral component of a system designed to achieve this important objective.

Another example of using technology to achieve an important educational objective can be found in the use of computer conferencing to network student teachers. We know from research and experience that student teachers need a strong support network. Unfortunately, the barriers of time and space have made it difficult to provide such networks that make possible the sharing of information, advice on immediate teaching problems, joint curriculum planning, etc. At the University of Northern Iowa this situation is compounded by the fact that student teaching is conducted in ten locations spread throughout the state. However, through the use of computer conferencing these student teachers and university field coordinators throughout the state can be linked with each other and to campus-based faculty to provide this important support network.

Numerous other examples could be given but suffice it to say that it is easier to implement an educational technology if that technology is being used directly as part of the solution to a clearly identified and important issue in education.

Design Structured Solutions

Although individual initiatives have been and always will be a key element in promoting the use of technology in education, the development of structured solutions to key issues that incorporate the use of technology into the plan can be an important factor in encouraging and supporting the use of technology. Individual initiative is a necessary but not sufficient condition for ensuring the use of technology within a social system.

By structured solutions, I mean a comprehensive plan to structure an environment in such a way so as to achieve an important educational goal. The plan we are implementing at the University of Northern Iowa to encourage minority youths to enter teaching is an example of such a structured solution to a key problem. As mentioned previously, the plan includes the identification of young people as early as the fifth and sixth grades who show an interest in and disposition toward teaching. This cohort group is then nurtured and socialized into the field of teaching throughout their precollegiate experience. Upon graduation from high school, they are admitted to UNI's teacher education program and provided financial support as needed to complete the program. The cohort group concept is maintained throughout their collegiate experience. The support structure continues for these new teachers during the first three years of teaching. An integral component of this structured solution to a problem is the use of computer conferencing to allow the various cohort groups to communicate with each other, for participants at different stages of the system, from beginning teacher to fifth grade student, to communicate, and for university and school personnel to be in constant communication with each other and with the student cohort groups.

This example illustrates the use of technology not as a stand-alone item, but as part of a larger structured solution to a real educational problem. The use of technology in this context transcends individual effort and incorporates the use of technology squarely into the achievement of a broad institutional objective.

Take a Systems Perspective

Given the complexity of promoting change within a highly complicated social system, it is little wonder that we as educators have a poor track record of creating integrated systems to achieve our objectives. The history of education is rife with examples of our inability or unwillingness to take a systems perspective toward educational change. The result is frequently frustration when good ideas fail, when some necessary part of the system does not support the change effort. Part of the problem is, of course, that what we call our educational system is not a system at all but instead a set of systems poorly connected. The large gap that exists between the systems of higher education and the systems of public and private elementary and secondary education is but one good example of multiple systems poorly linked. We would like to think of our institution of education as a large system tightly coordinated to achieve agreed upon objectives such as the broad utilization of technology in the nation's schools. In such a system, teachers, administrators, school boards, area educational agencies, state departments of education, governors, state legislatures, and universities would all pull together to achieve a common objective. Unfortunately, such a coordinated system does not exist.

But even when we do have an opportunity to take a systems perspective and structure the component parts of the system to empower for change, we frequently do not take that opportunity. For example, how many universities have purchased large amounts of technology for faculty use and then provided virtually no staff development in the use of this technology? Or how many school systems do you know that have purchased hands-on science curricular materials and then refused to provide adequate funds for maintenance and replacement or even storage of this equipment? These are but simple examples of our inability to take a systems perspective to facilitate change. Yet, as was pointed out in earlier sections of this chapter focusing on the importance of implementation and on structured solutions, a systems perspective is absolutely crucial if change is to be successful. All component parts of the system must be in place for full implementation to occur.

Expect Uneven Progress and Tolerate Ambiguity

Remember the old adage about the best laid plans. Regardless of how hard you try or how careful you are in planning, things will go wrong or at least differently than expected. Few things in life are linear and this is especially true when trying to bring about change in complicated social environments. If charted, the path toward your goal is at best zigzag and more likely than not marked by steps that appear to be in the wrong direction. At times, even the goal may seem to have lost its focus and become ambiguous. Accept these temporary sidesteps and setbacks. Learn as you go, stay flexible, but do not give up.

Use Time to Your Advantage

An important understanding in allowing one to continue in the face of adversity is that change is a process, not an event. Change takes place over time and sometimes over a long period of time. Accept the fact that you are in this for the long haul and plan for the change to occur in stages that take time. In an age of instant gratification, we sometimes feel, or may even be forced to feel, that we must demonstrate success almost immediately. This need for instant success, although somewhat a function of our culture, is unrealistic. Structure your solution, build the system, put the component pieces in place, and use time to your advantage.

Keep It Simple

In spite of my earlier recommendations to build structured solutions and to take a systems perspective, I sometimes feel that we make the whole process of change far too difficult. We do, of course, need to put all of the component pieces in place, but there is also a certain simplicity in bringing about change when one understands the human dynamics involved in the process. This understanding may be what comes from years of successful experience. Ron Lippitt, after spending his entire career considering the change process, expressed it so clearly one day when addressing a group of faculty members at the University of Michigan. He cautioned on starting change:

- Start with those who are ready.
- Mandatory change does not have a long life.
- Ambivalence and caution towards change are normal.
- Avoid the preoccupation with new goals without providing the methodology to achieve the goals.
- Avoid focusing on large gaps in "where we are" to "where we want to go."
- Take tiny steps and celebrate progress.
(Lippitt, 1980).

I have already commented in this chapter on several of these points. As Lippitt points out, mandatory change is likely to have a short life so you might as well start with those who are ready and build from that base. Accept that people will be cautious toward change, give them the tools necessary to achieve the change, and celebrate success along the way. I want to emphasize Lippitt's point concerning the importance of celebration. As you achieve success toward your goal, publicly celebrate. Acknowledge the good work of the people who are bringing the change along, and do it publicly. Hold a reception and invite others to attend. Conduct a press briefing, do a radio talk show. Find a way to celebrate the success you have had and let others know about it. A success story can go a long way toward building momentum for your change.

Put Someone in Charge

If you want change to occur, you must put someone in charge of the effort. Someone must wake up every morning thinking about what needs to be done to move the change process forward. Change does not occur by wishful thinking. Someone needs to be there to make it happen and to provide a support structure for others. This seems to be especially true when dealing with technology. For example, teachers in a school district attempting to implement the integration of microcomputers throughout the curriculum have often expressed the need for someone they could turn to immediately when they had a problem. People involved in a technological innovation, while dealing with all of the problems associated with any change, must also deal with the technology itself. For many people, the technology is a frightening component of the change effort. If the technology fails, they feel that they cannot fix it and want immediate help. In spite of this obvious need for someone to be in charge of the effort, it seems that many change efforts are not provided the leadership necessary to make it happen.

Make Technology Work for You in Multiple Ways

Computer conferencing is a good example of the use of a technology that can serve you in multiple ways. Once in place and accessible to multiple parties, its uses are only limited by the imagination. Messaging, problem solving, planning, simulations, sharing, curriculum development, course offerings, conferences, and departmental communications are only some of the applications of computer conferencing that have been described in this book. As more uses are made of technology, the cost per use decreases while its functioning becomes more integrated into the organization. The technology can no longer be seen as tangential to your efforts or as stand-alone pieces of equipment easily dispensed with when other priorities emerge.

Let Synergism Develop

With the type of systems perspective toward change being suggested here, where technology is ingrained within the system in multiple ways and is used to achieve multiple objectives, a synergistic effect can result. The total impact on the institution is far greater than the sum of the effects taken independently. In addition, the meaning of all this change on the institution as a whole may be quite different from what was intended as the result of any particular use of technology. Synergism may also provide a dynamic to the effort to infuse the use of technology throughout the system that gives the effort a virtual "life of its own." An enthusiasm can develop that is contagious and may bring the previously reluctant individuals into the network of adopters.

The Payoff Is in Social Change

Technological change is not synonymous with social change. It must be understood that adopting a new innovation in educational technology, although bringing a new tool into education, is not the change that is most important. The importance of the sheer use of the technology itself pales in comparison to the social changes that occur as a result of the use of the technology. The various uses of computer conferencing detailed in the previous chapters illustrate that the nature of human interaction changes as a result of the use of the conferencing systems. No longer constrained by the barriers of time and space, people are provided an interactive mode of communication not previously available to them. Problem solving takes on a new dimension when experts can use an interactive delphi technique to project directions for our future or when student teachers and their supervisors can bring their collective intelligence to bear on an immediate teaching problem or when students around the world can engage in an interactive simulation on a major world problem. In these cases the technology has served its purpose in allowing change to occur in the nature of human interaction. That change in human interaction is social change.

Understanding the human aspects of technological change helps us appreciate how individuals might be affected by the change and how they might react to the change. It also helps us understand the larger social consequences of the change we are attempting. And finally, it helps to keep us focused on the important aspects of the change—not the technology itself, but the social inventions we create around the technologies.

References

Bester, A. (1985). *Educational wastelands: The retreat from learning in our public schools*. Urbana, Ill: University of Illinois Press.

Bowden, R. (1988). Adaptation of employees to mandated integration of microcomputers in the workplace. Unpublished Doctoral Dissertation. Ann Arbor, MI: The University of Michigan.

Canning, C. (1988). Adoption of computing: The experience of six teachers. Unpublished Doctoral Dissertation. Ann Arbor, MI: The University of Michigan.

Federal Programs Supporting Educational Change. (1975). *Vol.1: A model of educational change*. Rand Corporation.

Letscher, J. (1982). Change and continuity: The ethos of three urban Catholic schools. Unpublished Doctoral Dissertation. Ann Arbor, MI: The University of Michigan.

Lippitt, R. (1980). Questions on starting a change process: Address to the faculty of the School of Education. Unpublished speech. Ann Arbor, MI: The University of Michigan.

Poppard, D. (1982). Job related stress and coping strategies as perceived by twelve principals of center city Catholic schools. Unpublished Doctoral Dissertation. Ann Arbor, MI: The University of Michigan.

Glossary

The following terms and phrases have been used in this book and may benefit from further elaboration.

Asynchronous

In the context of computer-mediated communication, this means the ability to communicate with other parties without having to be using the same medium at the same time. A message is sent and stored on a host computer system and then retrieved by the recipient at a later time.

Bulletin board system (bbs)

Computer software residing on a host computer that appends individual messages to each other around a topic. These kinds of systems are generally less sophisticated than computer conferencing systems. They are more likely found operating on an individual microcomputer and modem that are accessible by telephone one person at a time.

CompuServe

This is a commercial company that provides a range of information services, from data bases to communications facilities, on a fee basis.

Computer conferencing

Group discussion and private individual interaction that take place over computer-mediated communication networks. This is facilitated by sophisticated software residing on a host computer that is connected to one or more networks.

Following are five such systems mentioned in the book.

Caucus

A system developed by Charles Roth and marketed by Camber-Roth in Troy, New York. Its group discussion facility is in a linear item and response format that is very similar to the Confer style developed before it. It is the system in use at the University of Northern Iowa and the University of Virginia. It requires a Unix operating system to accommodate multiple users simultaneously, but is also available for one user at a time in a DOS environment.

Confer

One of the first better known systems, Confer was developed in the mid-1970s at The University of Michigan by Dr. Robert Parnes. It has been described as one of the most sophisticated of all the systems. Its development has been closely tied to the MTS operating system (see below) which has to date limited its portability to other types of computer systems.

CoSy

This system was developed at the University of Guelph in Canada in the 1980s. It is being used at the Open University in Milton Keynes, England.

EIES

This is one of the better known systems, along with Confer, developed in the mid-1970s at the New Jersey Institute of Technology by Dr. Murray Turoff.

Xbbs

This is an item-response type system similar to Caucus and Confer. It is used by the Big Sky Telegraph in Montana.

Electronic mail

The one-to-one communication of written text through a computer-mediated network. It is similar to the postal system in that correspondence originates with one person and travels to another through some transportation medium.

Local Area Network (LAN) See networks.

Modem

A device developed by the Bell Labs to modulate the digitized signal from the computer to travel over a telephone line that requires an analog signal. It is a shortened form of modulator-demodulator.

Michigan Terminal System (MTS)

A proprietary operating system developed at The University of Michigan in Ann Arbor. It is the operating system for Confer. Several universities around the world are users of this unique computing environment.

Networks

This is an encompassing term used to include a variety of uses. Simply, it represents the linking together of computers so that they can communicate with each other. A local area network (LAN) allows the high speed transmission of data among computers in a relatively small area in a relatively error free manner. A wide area network (WAN) is a communications system that covers a large area, perhaps hundreds or thousands of miles, using lines provided by a telephone company or other such common carrier. BITNET is one such network mentioned in this book. It links a number of universities around the world for the exchange of electronic mail. JaNET (Joint Academic Network) is a comparable network in Britain. Internet is a relatively new and more powerful network. Sponsored by the National Science Foundation, it is connecting to other smaller, regional networks (e.g., MIDNET in the Midwest) to facilitate the connection of educators at all levels, internationally.

Unix

This is a multiuser, multitasking operating system developed by AT&T. A number of variations have appeared and it has become very popular. Xenix, the Unix version developed by SCO in Santa Cruz, California, is the most common operating system for the Caucus computer conferencing system.

Resources

Some pertinent resources in print have been referenced in various chapters throughout this book. What follows is a selected list of people who have substantial experience with the use of computer conferencing in education. This list does not begin to be exhaustive. It only represents an assessment of people who have been active users of this technology for some time, as well as recommendations received from others.

Confer and EIES

The University of Michigan and the New Jersey Institute of Technology have, perhaps, the most substantial experience with this technology. Individuals at each of these institutions developed the major early computer conferencing systems in the mid-1970s. Following are key people associated with those developments.

Dr. Robert Parnes
Advertel Communications
2067 Ascot
Ann Arbor, MI 48103

Dr. Parnes created the Confer computer conferencing software at The University of Michigan in 1975. Since that time, its use has become widespread in higher education, business, and government.

Dr. Frederick L. Goodman
University of Michigan
4122 School of Education
Ann Arbor, MI 48103

He collaborated on the creation of Confer and on innovations in its use since 1975. He conceived and developed the Confer based Interactive Communications Simulations.

Dr. Karl Zinn
University of Michigan
Center for Research on Learning and Teaching
109 E. Madison
Ann Arbor, MI 48103

Dr. Zinn is a research scientist at The University of Michigan who has worked with computer conferencing since its inception at Michigan. He has helped innumerable individuals use this technology in various applications.

Dr. Murray Turoff
New Jersey Institute of Technology
Newark, NJ 07102

He created the Electronic Information Exchange System (EIES) in the mid-1970s, one of the best known of such systems used for extensive applications.

Dr. Starr Roxanne Hiltz
Upsala College
Department of Anthropology and Sociology
East Orange, NJ 07017

A sociologist who has collaborated with Dr. Turoff on the EIES system since its inception. She has contributed some of the most significant research on the characteristics and applications of this technology.

Other Resource People

Apart from the two institutions mentioned above, there are a number of other individuals across the country who have accumulated a variety of experiences with computer conferencing.

Dr. Glen Bull
University of Virginia
Curry School of Education
405 Emmet Street
Charlottesville, VA 22903

Dr. Bull has overseen the integration of this technology into the work of the University of Virginia, Curry School of Education. His institution and the University of Northern Iowa are perhaps the two leading examples of Schools and Colleges of Education using this technology in their work.

Dr. Christine Canning
University of Northern Iowa
511 Schindler Education Center
Cedar Falls, IA 50614

Dr. Canning's experience began at The University of Michigan and continues at the University of Northern Iowa, where she is using computer conferencing to develop collaborations with field based practitioners in the preparation of teachers.

Dr. John Clement
1112 Sixteenth Street, NW, Suite 600
Washington, DC 20036

Dr. Clement is working on a project for EDUCOM to develop an inclusive K-12 network aimed at facilitating curriculum reform and institutional restructuring.

Dr. Ward Deutschman
Dean of Telecommunications
New York Institute of Technology
Central Islip, NY 11722

Dr. Deutschman oversees the operation of the computer conferencing based distance delivery of college programs at NYIT American Open University.

Andrew Feenberg
Western Behaviorial Sciences Institute
LaJolla, CA 92093

Mr. Feenberg has been using this technology for most of the 1980s as part of the instructional program of the institute.

Dr. Lawrence B. Friedman
North Central Regional Educational Laboratory
1900 Spring Road
Oakbrook, IL 60521

Dr. Friedman studied the use of this technology in a rural teacher-researcher collaboration.

Mr. Anthony Kaye
The Open University
Institute of Educational Technology
Milton Keynes, England MK7644

Mr. Kaye's work at the Open University has resulted in important contributions to the literature on the uses of computer conferencing in distance education.

Dr. Frank Odasz
Western Montana College
Box 11
Dillon, MT 59725

Dr. Odasz has developed extensive applications on The Big Sky Telegraph serving rural educators and facilitating economic development.

Dr. Jean W. Pierce
Northern Illinois University
College of Education
DeKalb, IL 60115

Dr. Pierce helped initiate and maintain the networks for the American Educational Research Association and for educational researchers on BITNET and CompuServe.

Dr. Donald McNeil
Academy for Educational Development
1255 23rd Street NW
Washington, DC 20037

Dr. McNeil has extensive experience with distance education in various media, first as President of the University of Mid-America, using television and satellite delivery, and later, at the New York Institute of Technology, using computer conferencing.

Dr. Thomas J. Switzer
University of Northern Iowa
205 Schindler Education Center
Cedar Falls, IA 50614

Dr. Switzer has been using computer conferencing for ten years and has integrated it into his administration of the College of Education at the University of Northern Iowa, where he is Dean.

Dr. Michael D. Waggoner
University of Northern Iowa
510 Schindler Education Center
Cedar Falls, IA 50614

Dr. Waggoner was involved in teleconferencing in distance education while at the University of Alaska, Fairbanks. Since 1981, he has been involved with research and applications development in the use of computer conferencing, first at the University of Michigan and currently at the University of Northern Iowa.

Index